Xiao Hui Wang

Close to the Eyes

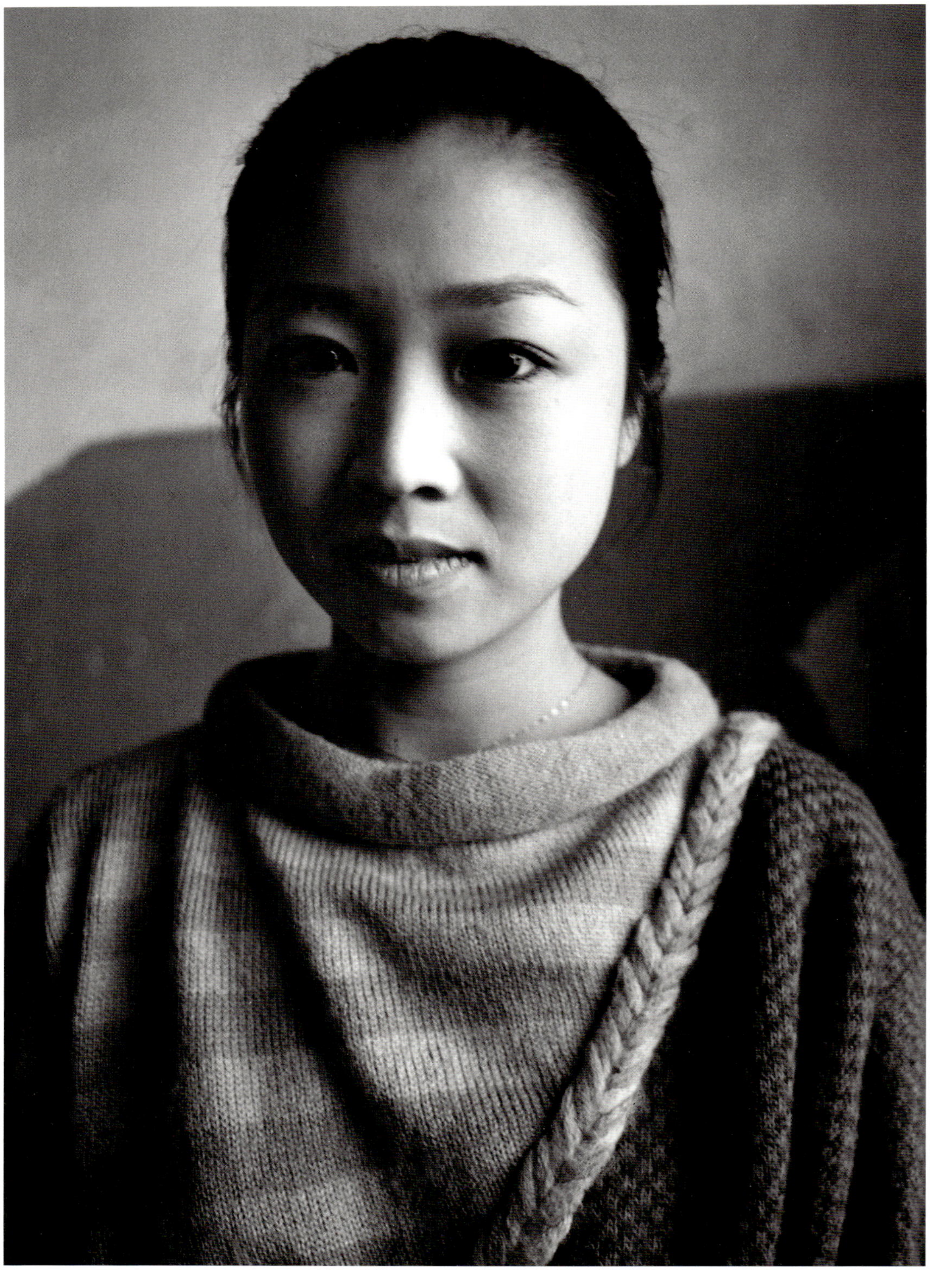

Close to the Eyes

The Portraits of Xiao Hui Wang

With texts
by Tilman Spengler and Xiao Hui Wang

Prestel
Munich · London · New York

This book has been published in conjunction with an exhibition held at the Versicherungskammer Bayern, Munich 6 Feb.–6 April 2002 (Curator: Marc Gundel) and at the Haus der Kulturen der Welt, Berlin Summer 2002 (Curator: Michael Thoss).

Front cover: Bangkok 1993
Page 2: Beijing 1994

Translated from the German by Christopher Jenkin-Jones
(*A Long Journey to Myself*)

Library of Congress Control Number: 2001093011

Die Deutsche Bibliothek
CIP-Cataloguing-in-Publication-Data is available

Prestel Verlag · Mandlstrasse 26 · 80802 Munich, Germany
Tel. +49 (89) 381709-0 Fax +49 (89) 381709-35

4 Bloomsbury Place, WC1A 2QA London, England
Tel. +44 (020) 7323-5004; Fax +44 (020) 7636-8004

175 Fifth Avenue, Suite 402, New York, NY 10010
Tel. +1 (212) 995-2720; Fax +1 (212) 995-2733

www.prestel.com

Prestel books are available worldwide.
Please contact your nearest bookseller
or one of the above Prestel offices
for details concerning your local distributor.

Editorial direction: Peter Stepan
Edited by: Christopher Wynne

Design and typography: Meike Weber
Lithography: Repro Ludwig, Zell am See
Font: Akzidenz Grotesk
Printed by: Sellier, Freising
Bound by: Conzella, Pfarrkirchen

Printed in Germany on acid-free paper

ISBN 3-7913-2485-3

Foreword

Xiao Hui Wang was first able to live out her passion for photography to the full in 1986. As a trained architect who had seen the first of her building projects realised in Shanghai, Wang travelled to Germany that year on a scholarship. The impressions she gained of her host country and her trips across Europe were captured in a series of photographs of town and country scenes composed along architectural and cinematic principles.

Her documentary pictures developed into art photography at the beginning of the 1990s. Xiao Hui Wang sharpened her eye by photographing herself in the months following a near-fatal car accident. From that point onwards, she took her camera with her everywhere. Like a visual diary, her photographs record events and moods.

The portrait photographs assembled here give an impression of Wang's art photography. Since 1994 she has photographed the people whose paths she has crossed on her travels through America, Asia and Europe: ordinary folk of different ages, occupations and backgrounds. Her sitters are apprehensive and shy, self-confident and enthusiastic; all of them reflect the authenticity of the moment and exude a certain sympathy. In an moment of intimacy Wang focusses on the most expressive features of a person's face: the stark contrasts of light and shade, the absence of a backdrop, and the focus on the eyes and the parts of the face "close to the eyes" reveal an almost unnerving proximity between the sitter and the observer.

The works collected in this volume are being shown at an exhibition at the Haus der Kulturen der Welt in Berlin. This is the second time that Xiao Hui Wang has been selected for this venue, the first being in 1993. As the artistic expressions of such a cultural ambassador, that is where they belong. It is therefore appropriate that, over the past 15 years, Munich and Shanghai have become Wang's bases and that a selection of her works are being shown at the Versicherungskammer Bayern in Munich as well.

Marc Gundel　　Michael Thoss

Reflex and Reflection
The Portraits of Xiao Hui Wang
Tilman Spengler

In China, gazing at a stranger might generally be considered rude. What's for sure though is the fact that, in classical Chinese art, the gaze is taboo. An object staring at the viewer is simply unthinkable. Characteristically, we would come across, say, the solitary gardener watching a bashful couple admiring a silky cat that has its eyes fixed on a beautiful bird. Thus, we have various viewpoints and bearings, but nothing that crosses the imaginary line separating a work of art from its viewer.

The portrait is an exception, although in China, the genre is not regarded as art, which is why portraits usually lack signatures. Portraits of the imperial family or of someone's ancestors draw distinctive bonds, so, speaking in European terms, they are religious items.

In everyday life though, the Chinese tend to deal much more liberally with the gaze. At least this is what we learn from travellers ever since the country has been travelled: foreigners find themselves the target of an almost poetical curiosity. The length of someone's nose is acknowledged just as much as their eye colour, the shape of their forehead and chin, the chubbiness of their cheeks and the abundance or lack of hair on their heads. The foreigner's first reaction was acute irritation, but, on growing accustomed to it and eventually returning home, he would come to miss this unusual kind of attention. Which goes to show that curiosity certifies sympathy, whereas going unnoticed is proof of indifference. Early Chinese travellers to Europe or America in fact made similar experiences.

In traditional Chinese culture, the culture of Xiao Hui Wang, foreignness usually aroused suspicion, despite the tales of mythical kingdoms beyond the country's borders, and Buddhism brought to China from India, and music from Korea, and highly valued goods from distant places. But more often, foreigners were 'savages', 'barbarians' from all over the world and a menace to decency and peace. To put it bluntly, they represented *nature* in the midst of a world of *culture*. In 14th century images, barbarians were headless, or depicted as creatures with grotesquely lengthened ears or perforated bellies where a rod could be inserted for transportation.

This was a melting pot of myths, fairy tales, collective nightmares and phobias that vanished in the face of factual political threats. These threats arose in the mid 19th century, when European and then Japanese imperialism set out to dismantle the empire. Under communist rule, especially under Mao's 'Cultural Revolution' between 1966 and 1976, foreignness was universally demonized. Even portraits of Marx, Lenin and Stalin, as far as they were still around, had a slightly Asian touch. There has hardly been an unobstructed Chinese view on foreigners ever since.

The photographer Xiao Hui Wang belongs to the vanguard of a generation which has freed itself of ideology. With the curiosity bequeathed on her by her culture, and with the frankness of the artist, she overrules foreigness by uninhibitedly gazing. Her subjects are aquaintances from all over the world. Perhaps we can sense what kind of people they are, which country or social strata they come from, whether they are Bedouins, fashion designers, munks, gigolos or princesses, but that is not the point. What is important is the attention the photographer pays to her subjects, and vice versa. We seem to bear witness to a single moment of attention. But in this single moment, the viewer and the pictures interact: there is a reflex, a mutual reflection.

Are the sitters posing? A little maybe, since they aren't actors. Their slight awkwardness, the seconds of tenseness in their faces, the way they place their hands and bend their necks tells us so much about them. We can hardly imagine Xiao Hui Wang appearing on the scene as the glamorous photo artist, or sneaking up on people like an undercover agent. She openly admits to being curious, allowing sitters to smooth down their hair and straighten their blouses, to remove their pipes and cigarettes – but avoiding accuracy or exaggeration. And this leads us back to the aspect of cultural history: finding a balance between nature and culture.

Xiao Hui Wang's work focuses on the eyes we look at, and the eyes that look at us, the eyes that help us perceive the strangers in front of us. In Chinese, the eyes are known not to imbibe, but to piece together – or to refrain from piecing together, if there is too much to see at once. A person lacking self-awareness is known as someone whose eyes fail to see his own eyelashes. Xiao Hui Wang's portraits are masterpieces of piecing together. They make us see the strange and the familiar. And more than once, encouragingly, there is the hint of a smile.

A Long Journey to Myself

Xiao Hui Wang

A journalist once wrote that to hear my story one would think I was at least a hundred years old. Another newspaper reported me as having "seven lives".

I was born in early summer 1957 in the north Chinese seaport of Tianjin. It is the third largest city in the country and is situated some two hundred kilometres south of Beijing.

At the age of twenty, my mother already had four children. She wanted to study music but had been forced to marry her brother-in-law when she was sixteen, her sister having died after giving birth to two children. On the day my mother's first child was born, the eight-year Sino-Japanese war broke out. Fleeing thousands of kilometres from the Japanese troops, her first husband and three of her children died. My two cousins and half-brother survived. After the war my mother had to work extremely hard to feed her children and could only study music much later, with my father's help. They met shortly before the People's Republic was declared in 1949. He had just turned nineteen and was eight years younger than my mother.

My mother was thirty six when I was born. In her eyes my birth was a "stroke of luck", for not only my existence but her being pregnant helped ward off persecution. It was 1957, the time of the "Anti-Right Movement". Thousands of intellectuals faced a dire fate. In most cases final safety came only two decades later. She was teaching at the Music Academy in Tianjin. Two years earlier, in the drive against the counter-revolutionaries, she had spent a long year in captivity, unsure whether she would survive. She had been accused of spying for the Kuomintang. My father was the only person who stood by her during this desperate time. He wrote to her daily despite massive Party pressure to leave her, knowing his letters were being opened and read. After her release and the longed-for reunion with my father, my mother became pregnant. The name my father chose for me echoed hers, for her name is Hui Lin. It means "forest of wisdom". Xiao Hui is "the small wisdom".

On a child's first birthday in China a game is played to "predict" the future. On my first birthday, my parents, grandmother and youngest aunt were in the house. They can still recall many details of the game to this day. A range of objects like pencils, a doll, coins, a lipstick, toys and sweets, were spread out on a bed. Somehow it was conveyed to me I was allowed to pick out only one thing. I crawled around inspecting the objects with great interest, but I did not want any of them. They pressed me to take something, and finally I reached out for the object furthest away from me — a picture book.

Everyone laughed, saying here was one more person in our family who was interested in books. The tradition of teaching extended through three generations on my mother's side: my maternal grandfather taught literature at teachers' training college, my mother taught composition at the Music Academy, and my brother was teaching maths at a grammar school then. The path seemed to be marked out for me as well.

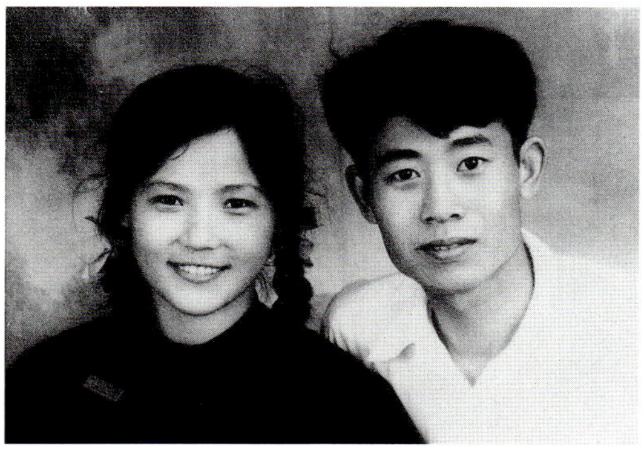

My mother Hui Lin Xü and my father Feng Wang
in 1953, the year of their wedding.
She was 32, he was 24 years old.

Until I was thirty and older, the forecast verified itself. I took a degree in China, did an extension course, taught architecture in Shanghai, and later, in Germany, I began to write my doctoral thesis and lecture on Chinese architecture and landscape gardening. To this day books play a big role in my life. Since arriving in Germany fifteen years ago, I have produced a book a year on average, most of them with photographs. It does indeed seem that my life refers back to that game.

Had my father lived in the West he would certainly have become a wealthy man. One of the youngest engineers in China, he was responsible for many new inventions, which he could not patent, however, because there were no patent protection laws. His exceptional professional success would soon be held against him. It was no secret that he adored his only daughter. His friends pulled his leg, saying that if Xiao Hui were to ask for the moon, he would go and fetch a ladder for her to climb up to it.

My father attended scrupulously to all the practical details of my upbringing, while my mother saw to it that I received adequate "spiritual nourishment". During the Cultural Revolution I was the only person she could confide in, and although I was still only a child, she told me everything without reserve.

An early experience may show how special our relationship was. Six days of the week I was at kindergarten. Only on Sunday was I allowed to go home. A lot of the children in my group contracted a scalp disease, and we were told the virus would only respond to x-ray treatment. We all lost our hair. In many cases it did not regrow. When I started going to school I had to wear an awful wig, and of course the other kids made fun of me. After a while I could bear it no longer. I went to my mother, had a good cry, and told her I did not want to go to school any more. She told me the tale of the Ugly Duckling. She said that not physical beauty but virtue, knowledge, abilities, in other words the inner human values, were what really counted. And she warned me that beautiful girls often neglected to form and refine their characters.

After this I worked doubly hard at school, and I always got the maximum grade of 100 in all subjects. This earned me great respect in everyone's eyes. A year later a miracle occurred. My hair began to grow again. To everybody's amazement it grew in light curls, rare in China, and it made me more popular than ever. The "ugly duckling" had vanished. These events taught me the value of perseverance and patience for the first time in my life. They helped me cope with more difficult situations later on. For many other stumbling blocks were to materialize along my way.

When I was small everyone said I was going to be a musician. Long before I could speak a complete sentence, so I am told, I could note every tune I heard. At five, I began taking piano lessons. Living in the Music Academy gave me ready access to the best teacher. My talent was universally praised, and — like my parents — I was sure I would later become a musician.

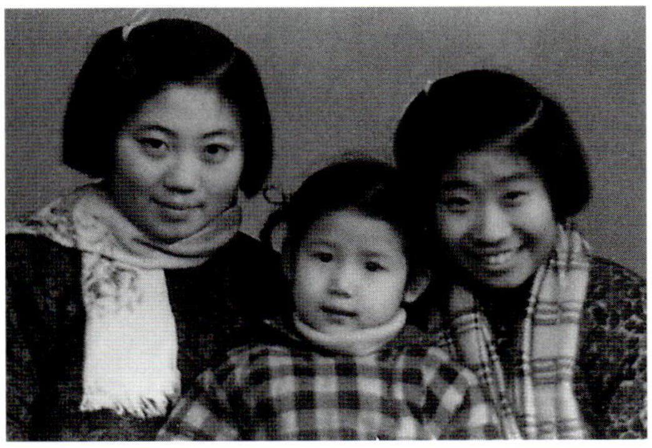

Sitting between two of my aunts.

But, beginning in 1966 when I was nine, the Cultural Revolution put an end to my mother's hopes for me once and for all. Books and music were burnt, and records thrown in the river, so as to give the Red Guards no excuse for destroying our remaining possessions. My parents had to separate because my mother, having close relatives in Taiwan, was suspected once again of spying. They wished to help me and prevent me from being sent off to the countryside. The Music Academy was shut down. I moved to my father's.

Nightfall on Sundays was the time when I would visit my mother secretly. It was her favourite time of the week, and her little room was filled with happiness.

However, my father's separation from my mother did not cause the revolutionaries to relent one bit in their degrading treatment of him, which included physical abuse. News-sheets bearing accusations against him were even posted on our front door. The neighbours' children were all told not to play with me.

Expelled from the best school in town, I was sent to another, where I had to clean the classroom before dawn and write the latest propaganda slogans up on the board. In winter it was my job to clean and light the stoves. I had to do more and harder menial work than the other children, because of my background. We belonged to the so-called "black families". The "red families" ostracized us. Luckily, there were some older neighbours who sympathized with us. Now and then they would slip me a titbit.

"It is better to die on one's feet than to live on one's knees," an old Chinese proverb says. My father could no longer bear the humiliating treatment and injustice. As he saw it, his continued existence could only make my life more difficult, and he decided to put an end to his own. He wrote farewell letters to my mother and to a cousin my mother had brought up, asking her to take me in. She lived with her family in Beijing and was a daughter-in-law of the former Minister of Culture, Mao Dun, one of China's most famous and influential writers, and one of the very few intellectuals and artists to receive protection under Mao and Zhou Enlai. My father hoped that this might improve my chances in life.

I was at my grandfather's on the evening of my father's suicide attempt. Lying in bed, I could hear the two men talking for a long time. Finally, my father took his leave. He was going to electrocute himself. However, at the critical juncture, a power cut hit our district — a frequent occurrence then — and my father was thwarted in his plan. He saw this later as a sign from the gods to go on living for me. Apart from the two personal farewell letters, he had also sent a critical document to his labour unit repudiating all the allegations against him, which, of course, only exacerbated his situation now. The next day, they came and fetched him. It was a long time before he returned home. My cousin, who had come especially from Beijing, discovered to her great relief that he was still alive. My grandfather gained permission to visit him occasionally in the labour camp. My parents would not let me go along with him.

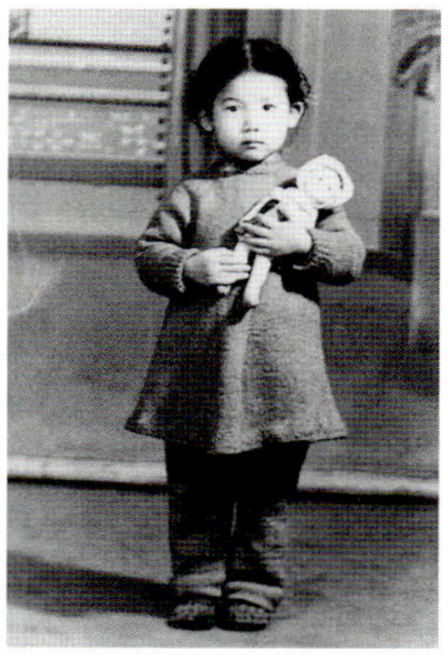

Aged 4 with my favourite doll.

"Red category" folk shunned us, while those of the "black category" feared too much contact. Once — it was the moon festival, an important occasion for friends, family and relatives to re-unite — my mother and I visited a friend. Those present look at the moon together and remember those who are absent. Seen thus the moon is a symbol of union. In ancient China, scholars would sit up drinking wine on this eveningand may have played a game of forfeits. Each guest had to continue a poem started by someone else, and if the others were not satisfied, he had to drain his glass. Our friend had been denounced as a counter-revolutionary. Diaries had been discovered at his home in which he had set down his thoughts on the Cultural Revolution. We only had tea, not wine, and just a small moon cake. His girlfriend recalls me cutting the little puff-pastry cake into four equal pieces and then, to everyone's delight, sharing out the crumbs as well. In our game of forfeits I always began. I still recall my mother saying: "We are drinking a glass of Nothing together". It described our situation perfectly in Zen-Buddhist terms. We were trying to compensate for the hollowness of the external world and for our persecution by giving our inner world spiritual meaning. As my mother said, it is easy to put a finger through a paper window; but if a finger is at the same place on the other side, it is no longer possible.

My personal situation improved slightly. Although I had to perform all the same menial tasks, I earned some respect by working hard. Cultural life then was more or less non-existent; a few propaganda plays and films, including Russian films on Lenin, and Albanian works, could be seen. We occasionally copied out forbidden literature and circulated it secretly. Being caught would certainly have meant severe punishment.

It was our great chairman's idea that all children of university-going age should leave the cities for retraining in the country and to share the hardships of rural life, unsure whether they would ever return. The only way out was, if one had some artistic talent, to work in a propaganda troupe, touring from village to village and performing. I became an accordion player. I practised for hours daily. My trousers wore through at the thighs. Even if we were expected to be "revolutionary", it was fun for me to be creative if only in small ways, writing playlets, directing and acting as well. My plays sometimes came in for criticism as not "revolutionary" enough, and too romantic. Yet they were generally popular. Creativity was also tolerated in cooking, although many basic foodstuffs were strictly rationed. Sometimes I remodelled the dresses we were no longer allowed to wear. Of course, there was no question of showing these creations off in public.

My real passion was photography even at this time. When I was thirteen a friend gave me a home-made "viewer", a wooden box with an electric bulb and a sheet of glass for the negatives. It was a primitive enlarger. To me it was a piece of magic. It almost became an addic-

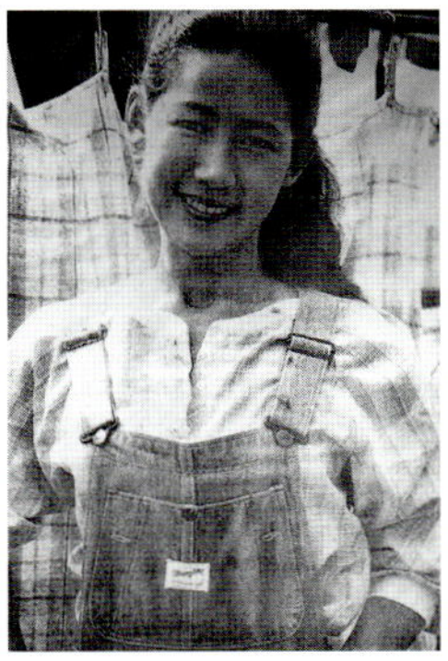

Just before leaving Shanghai
for Europe, summer 1986

tion. Night after night I "viewed" all the negatives we could find. My friend managed to get hold of some old photographic paper. Sometimes we would move the negative and produce outsized eyes or overlong legs.

My first proper camera dates from this time. To begin with it was only on loan from my uncle. He was an architecture professor. He taught me how to use it, and further stimulated my interest in photography. Seeing how fascinated I was, my father gave me a Chinese medium-format camera. He still recalls taking me on his motorbike on the National Holiday that year, camera in one hand, stool in the other, to shoot the firework display over the big bridge. The stool was our tripod. My father had to shout out the exposure times. Developing the film was more primitive still. We had no developing chamber, no darkroom. At night, a washbowl was set on the floor, chemicals poured in, and the film drawn through until it was uniformly bathed in developer. After a while, I would switch on a torch covered with red paper to see if it had had long enough. Such were the beginnings of my "career" as a photographer thirty years ago.

Music and photography brightened my life no end. They were the oasis at the midst of what otherwise was a cultural desert. They were also an outlet for one young being's accumulated energies and creativity.

The end of the Cultural Revolution is linked in my mind with the earthquake of 1976. On July 28th, a violent earthquake shook Tangshan, not far from my home town, killing over three hundred thousand people. Our house was demolished. My mother and I were able to get out just in time. Some young friends helped me recover our most valuable possession, the piano, from under the rubble. But aftershocks were feared, and in the general panic and hurry no one thought to rescue my negatives.

The same friends helped me build a temporary house, propped up against a wall opposite a refuse collection point. Our electricity came from the nearest street lamp. The street being narrow, lorries often drove past so close that occasional damage was inevitable. When this happened I was the repair girl, for apart from my mother no one else was around. Once I was fixing our cardboard roof when a good friend chanced by, Feng Jicai. He was later to become one of China's leading writers. In his short novel, *The Song of the Boat*, he describes our life then, putting my roof repairs in a very poetic light: "In the light of early summer, a slip of a girl is sitting up on a roof. Cooing doves are whirring around her." I did not find the situation romantic at all. I felt miserable, despairing, dirty, and I wished someone would help me.

On 9th September 1976, Mao died. Some weeks later, the Gang of Four were arrested. The Cultural Revolution came to an end. When Deng Xiaoping returned to power, he re-introduced a general university entrance exam. For ten years, admittance to universities had been restricted to the so-called "three red generations", who had

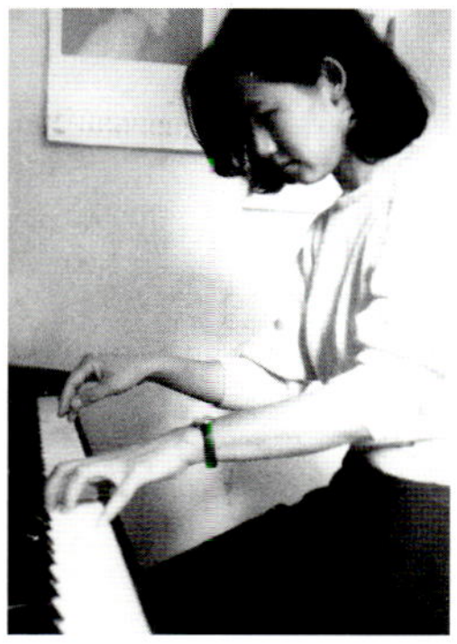

The piano was a wedding present to me from my father. It had been my parents' hope and my childhood dream that I would become a musician.

Entrance to the Islamic restaurant in Shanghai (1986), which I designed as an architect.

My abstract ink paintings.

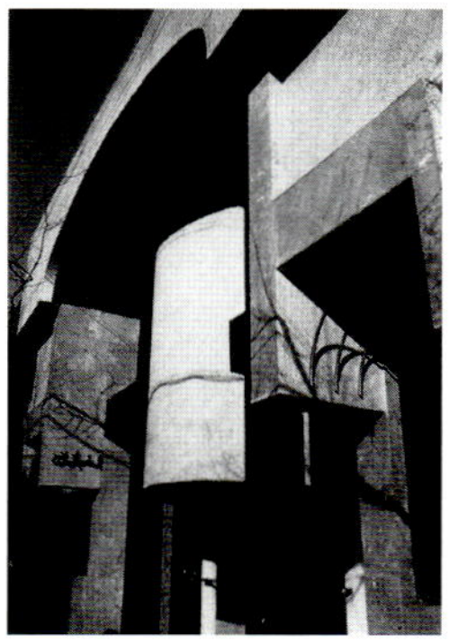

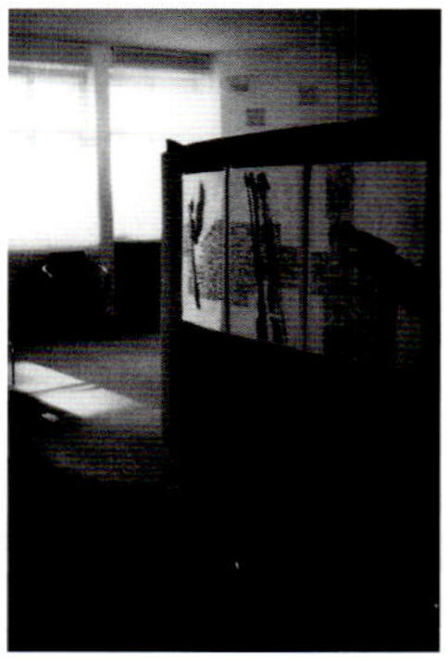

been able to attend a rudimentary course "on recommendation". For many young people now was the chance to return to the cities. Of twelve million applicants, only 2.5% actually got a place. Colleges and academies connected with the arts remained closed, and as my heart was set on the High School for Film, I decided to wait a year. My father said I should take the exam now, as there was no knowing what the future would bring. My mother was against an artistic career. In her experience of China, it meant risking one's life. She wanted me to do something practical. My uncle suggested architecture because, of all technical subjects, it was closest to art. I burnt the candle at both ends preparing for the exam, for I was also competing against people who had prepared for it ten years earlier, with a much better education than we had had during the Cultural Revolution. I applied to three universities. All were ready to take me. Although the Tongji University, Shanghai, was the furthest from Tianjin, I chose it because it had the best Architecture Faculty. Founded by Germans ninety years ago, it is still one of the country's top universities. I spent nine years at the Architecture Faculty even though in my second year there the High School for Film re-opened. I could have studied alongside Zhang Yimo and Chen Kaige. I have often chafed at my parents' "good sense".

I did not forget my photographic interests at Tongji University. I was one of the first members of a newly-founded students' Photographic Society. We received good equipment to work with, and in return we did photo-journalistic work for the university. Our supervisor, Professor Jin Jing Chang, who had studied in Germany before the war and specialized in photographing urban architecture, later gave his collection to the Deutsches Museum, Munich. He taught us the handicraft of the professional photographer.

In the vacations I travelled around, taking pictures of people and countryside. Photography was not popular at all in China at the time and few families possessed a camera. It was then that I met my future husband Yu Lin.

Although China was opening up in the late 1970s, travel abroad was still very much the exception. In 1979, a one-year grant was offered to study at the Academy of Art, Vienna. Two candidates were to be selected from our faculty, first to learn German for a year. Then one of them was to be chosen to go to Europe. Yu Lin and I were the two candidates. Although we were competitors, we liked each other a lot. For some reason, a few months later a different student was chosen, someone who already had a degree in German. We did our best to renew contact to our fellow students. We were studying together a lot now and came closer. The chance of an overseas grant did not arise again for six years. I finished studying, did my three-year extension course, and began working at the university as an assistant. Years later we could see that that missed opportunity had been our gain. For only in this way had we really got to know each other.

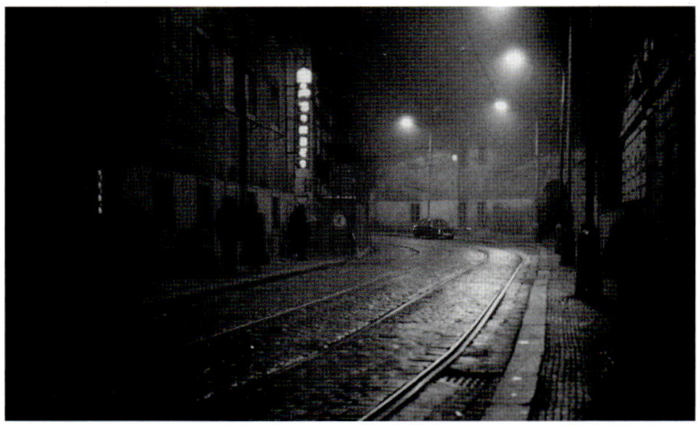
Prague 1988

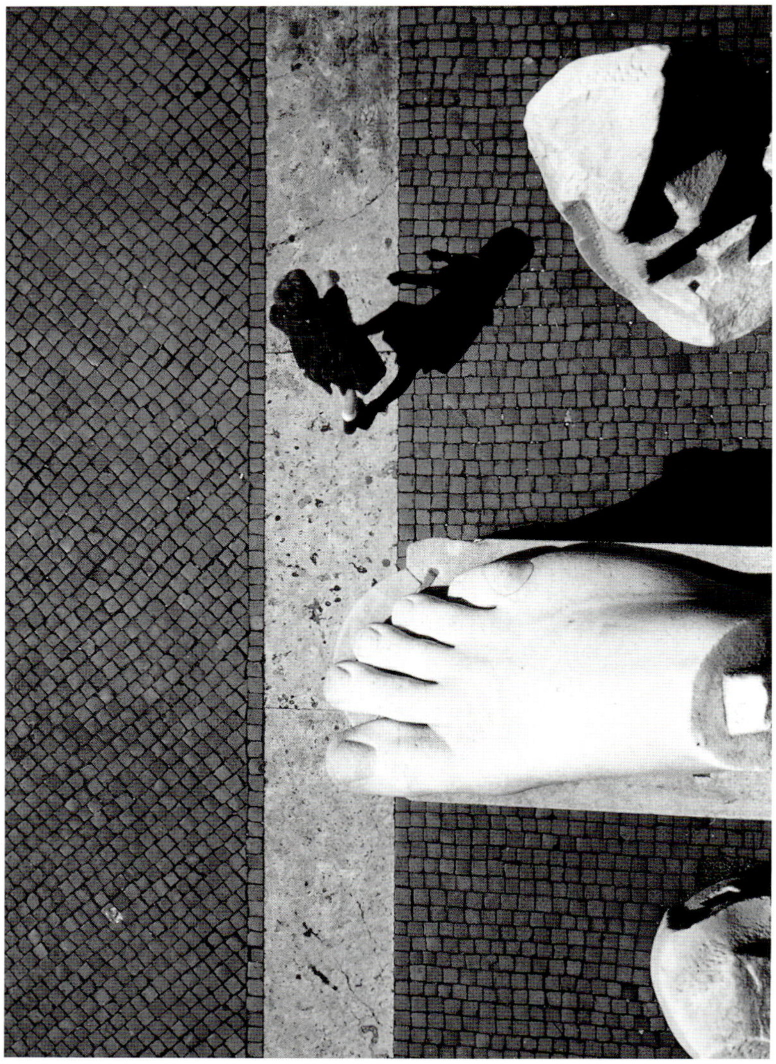

Rome 1987

Architecture interested me, and I took pleasure in leading some projects. However, other souls dwelt in my breast. My real dream was to make my own films. After moderating a programme on world famous architecture for Shanghai television, I received various offers to work as a film actress. This seemed one way of getting into the film world. But then I applied for, and was awarded, a German grant. It was especially attractive as it included numerous trips to study European architectural history at original sites. This time my parents' advice was sound. And so, in October 1986, I came to Munich.

A day before leaving for Germany, Yu Lin and I married. We had deliberately been putting it off since married couples were not allowed to leave the country together. Lin too had received a prestigious grant, in his case to study in Berlin. On my study trips in Europe I photographed architecture, cities and landscapes, almost exclusively in colour. For the first time in my life I could be lavish with film. In China a Kodak slide film with development had cost almost as much as my assistant's monthly salary at the Tongji University, and I had had to consider very carefully before pressing the button. Before I left for Europe, my writer friend Feng Jicai said there were two things I should not stint on — films and stamps.

The first months in the new and unfamiliar world were phenomenally exciting. In spring 1987, I stood on Venice's Piazza San Marco for the first time in my life — known to me until then only from a drawing at school — wondering if it was a dream or reality. Years earlier, it would never have entered my head that I might actually be there one day in person, not even in a dream. I soaked up new impressions like a sponge, but I could not assimilate them, so I began recording my experiences in a diary. Since then it has become my constant companion. Without these diaries I would never have been able to write *My Visual Diary – 15 Years Living in Germany*, which is due out in China this autumn. Leafing through all the little notebooks, many forgotten details came back.

Lin was deeply in love with me. An accomplished calligrapher, he once did a large rendering of the character "Hui", writing next to it "this character stands for wisdom, but for me it means much more". He had painted his favourite characters in large calligraphic strokes even as a student. It requires a great deal of skill and concentration, as everything must be done in one freehand movement, without lifting brush from paper. He frequently drew the character for "dream" in an unusual, light-grey colour that brought out the word's emotional connotations.

But the way Lin sacrificed his career out of love for me was more unusual. One of a small group of academics, I had come to Europe on a one-year grant, and the time for my return was nearing. Lin, on the other hand, had been awarded a further grant to continue his doctoral thesis under Max Baecher at the University of Darmstadt. He decided to turn it down and return to China with me. It was no easy decision. He was not only turning down a grant; a doctorate from a

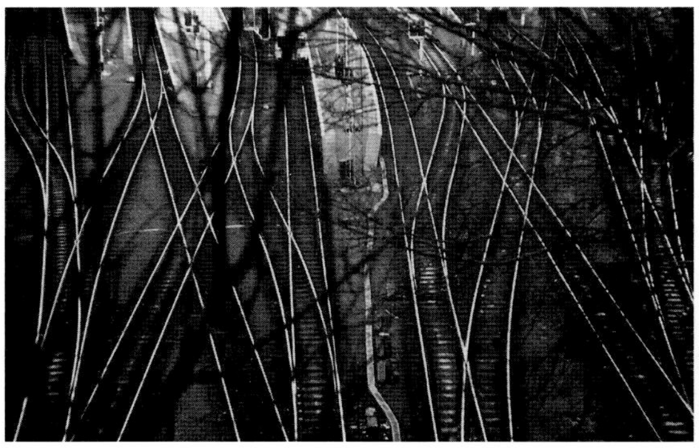

Edinburgh 1987. My father once said that this photo symbolizes my life: many lines cross and dissect each other.

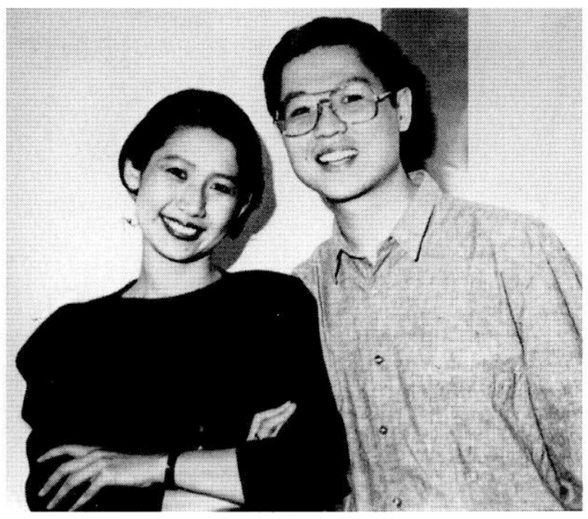

In Munich with my husband Lin Yu, 1989 who was killed in a car accident in 1991

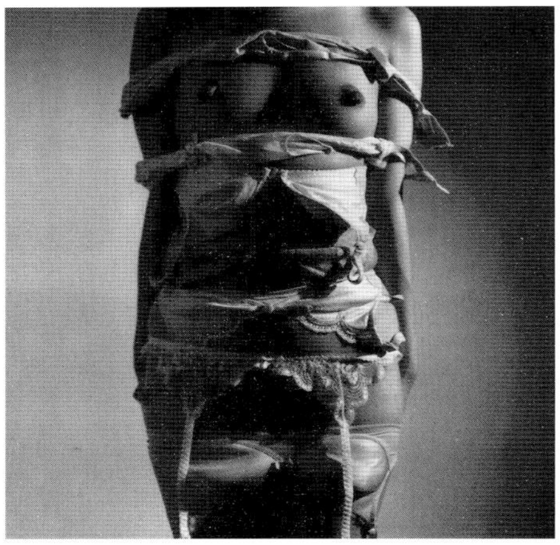

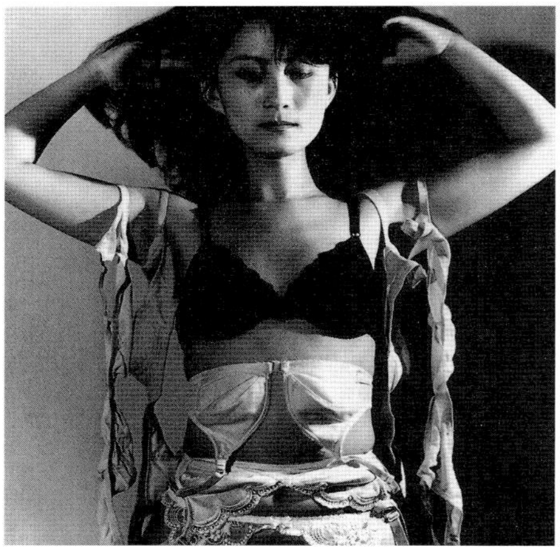

"Partly freed woman No. 1 and No. 2", 1991

German university would have given him automatic professorship at a Chinese university, with all the amenities such as a flat, interesting architectural work and much else besides. Or his returning with me might be held against him as "spinelessness" or "failure". Again, we could only apply for an overseas stay once every five years. There was no guarantee such an opportunity would arise again.

I was unable to opt out of the group and stay in Germany as I was under great political pressure. On the other hand, I had taken – secretly – and passed the preliminary examination to start work on a doctoral thesis at the Technical University, Munich. Professor Wienands, my future supervisor, had even offered me a job. All this was wishful thinking though. I had no option but to keep in with the group.

A tragic event changed everything. On the day we were due to depart, a good friend of mine committed suicide out of frustrated love for me. When I had acquired enough distance to this loss many years later, I wrote a film script called *Burnt Out Blue Candle*, in which I tried to record the unhappy melodramatic encounter in memory of him. Although he was probably unaware what his deed would trigger off, he did indirectly fulfil his wish to keep me in Germany. For as a result of the ensuing police investigations, Lin and I had to remain in the country to begin with.

At Munich University, I started to work on a doctoral thesis: "The Intellectual and Spiritual Background of Classical Chinese Architecture". It was no easy choice compared to the alternative of

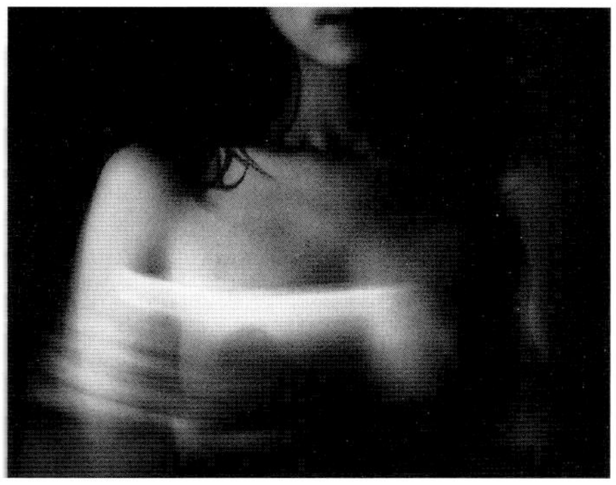

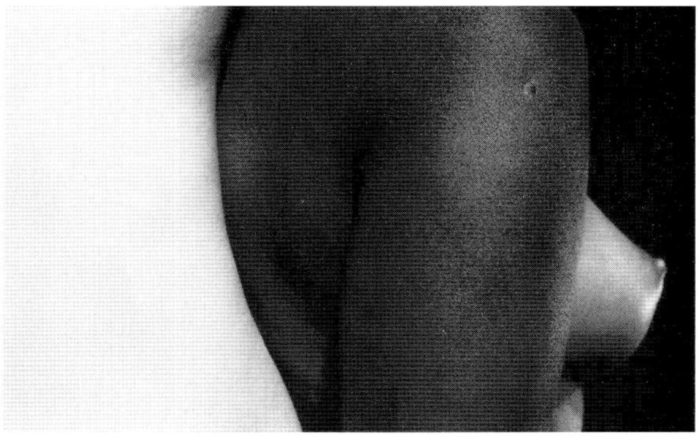

"Attempting to take the precious No. 2", 1990. This picture expresses my feelings when I had to leave my home country.

"Male left, female right" from the Yin-Yang Series No. 9, 1990 continuing my old subject at Tongji University: "Visual Information and its Communication". It was paradoxical. In China, Western culture interested me more than anything else, whereas in Europe I felt the need to trace ancient Chinese traditions. Shortly after, I began teaching the subject at the Architecture Faculty.

A Christmas present from Lin set me on a new and unexpected path, which took me away from academic life. He had enlarged my best slides from our Europe trips and mounted them on large cardboard sheets. Friends in Munich spontaneously suggested putting on a private exhibition in their house during the holidays. I never thought so many artists would praise my work. Many of them said I ought to become a professional. I would never have dared to take this path alone. A good friend took me to the Book Fair, and four publishers expressed interest. This was the beginning of the two books *Home of the Dragon* and *Munich – Seeing and Experiencing*, the latter my first commissioned work as a photographer.

In time, more and more commissions from publishers came in, especially for books on cities and landscapes. I travelled widely and enjoyed it. But I had to husband my time carefully, for I had also enrolled as a student at the High School for Television and Film. Lin and I had now received an unlimited residence permit, he was working as an architect in an established office, and he encouraged me to follow my heart. In the end, in October 1991, I decided to give up my teaching jobs. A day after my last day at work, Lin and I drove to Prague to take photos for a new book. But we never arrived; for in a tragic car accident my husband lost his life, while I was severely injured.

Lin was thirty-four years old. People who knew him know how warm-hearted and loveable he was. The rector of Tongji University had once said he had met such talent in students only very rarely. The leading architect in the office where he had worked described him as "the most talented and imaginative of workers, he contributed enormously". His supervisor, Professor Baecher, wrote that "no one was more intelligent, friendly, cheerful, loveable and talented, no one represented his country and its youth, with his personality or so positively, as he did. What a shame it is not known in your country what an important representative he was of your people, your culture and your country. Lin should receive an award for all he has done for China over here".

Lin's life was like the "dream" character he had drawn, only his life had been more vibrant and colourful than that grey sign. When we had first been in love in 1981, he presented me with a book he had made, using photos of me. On the first page, he wrote: "The dream one sees with closed eyes is soon forgotten – the one that one experiences with open eyes stays in the heart – and will remain there, until breath stands still".

After his death my mother asked why, in his happiest moments, he had alluded to tragedy in this way. His dream was over now. For me it was also like an incomprehensible dream, or a nightmare.

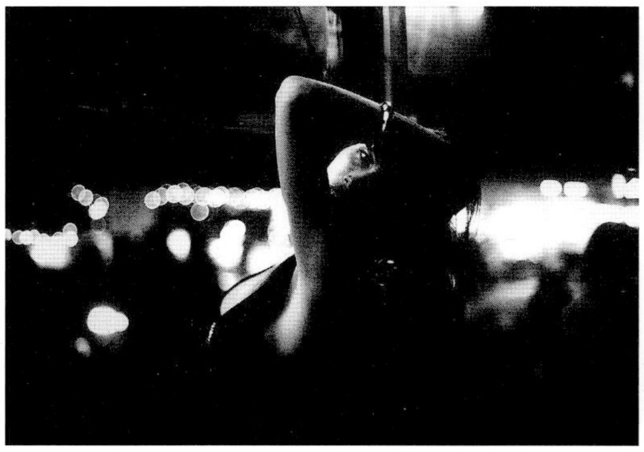

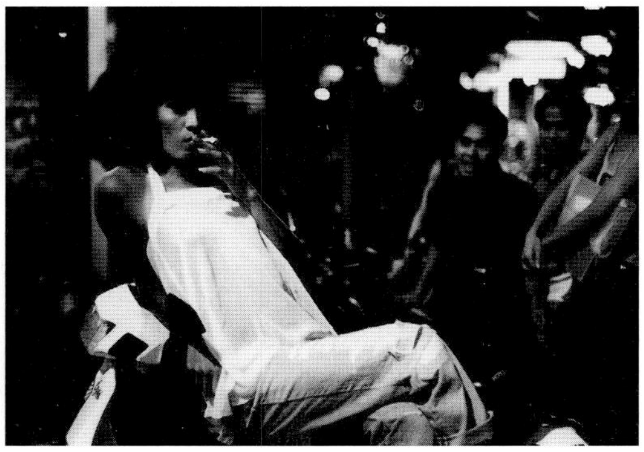

"Koh Samui street and nightscene", Thailand 1993

"Pataya – woman on a motorbike", Thailand 1993

In the entrance exam for the High School for Television and Film, I had written a film exposé on two contrasting ideas of love. The one is passionate, like fire; it brooks no opposition, and simply sucks one in. But fire flares and then goes out. The other kind of love is like air. It is around one all the time, invisible, one cannot even feel it. That is why one is often unaware of its existence. But if the air disappears, breath stands still. This is how I felt after losing Lin.

I spent agonizing weeks in hospital, fully conscious of my loss, unable to move, my body injured and soul wounded. I had no idea how my life could continue. It was terrible. I also had plenty of time to reflect. In all the preceding years, I had been so busy and spent too little time on this. I wrote my thoughts down in my diary, they could no longer be ignored: emotions, relationships, death. Having narrowly escaped death myself, I became intensely interested in religion and fate. For six months I was off work. To begin with I was at a complete loss. Without the warm-hearted aid of many friends it would have been more difficult still. I am immensely grateful to them. There were often very moving moments when they helped me feel I was not alone.

An exhibition of my photographs entitled *My 24 Hours* was scheduled for around this time. Through my various activities and roles at the High School for Television and Film, the Architecture Faculty, in publishing, and my photographic work, my days were kaleidoscopic. I was also collaborating on film projects at various locations. I began to keep my camera with me at all times, for personal use, and over the years I put together a sort of visual diary.

Even in hospital before I could sit up, I was photographing friends, doctors and nurses. I photographed myself – my scarred face, my eyes full of sadness. I was no pretty sight. But the honesty of the moment was crucial. I was beginning to see that truth is all-important, whether in art or in life.

I am, basically, an emotional person. A review of my first book of photographs bore the title "The world as seen by the heart". I wished to use the lens to think and to penetrate through layers of feeling to deeper regions of life. Previously I had photographed objects, sometimes abstractly, sometimes more surrealistically, and had sought a fundamentally aesthetic experience. The traumatic experience of the accident shifted people to the centre of my work. Outer forms became less important. Now it is much more a question of human existences, the circumstances of people's lives, and the moments of face-to-face encounter.

The French writer Romain Rolland has compared life to a swinging pendulum, with happiness and grief at the extremities of its swing. You cannot make the pendulum stop at one extreme. For the artist, suffering is often a creative source. When I was still small, my mother used to say bodily pain is easier to bear than mental pain. Mental pain, she said, was like the sea, bitter and boundless. As a child, I could not understand this. I once read in a biography of Van Gogh how his teacher said to him, "To experience suffering, and not happi-

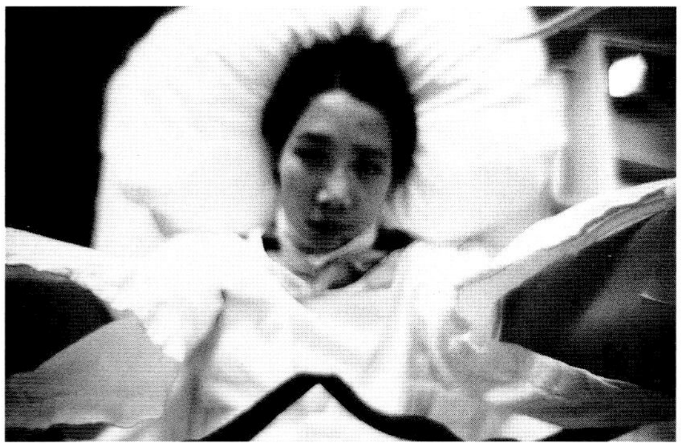

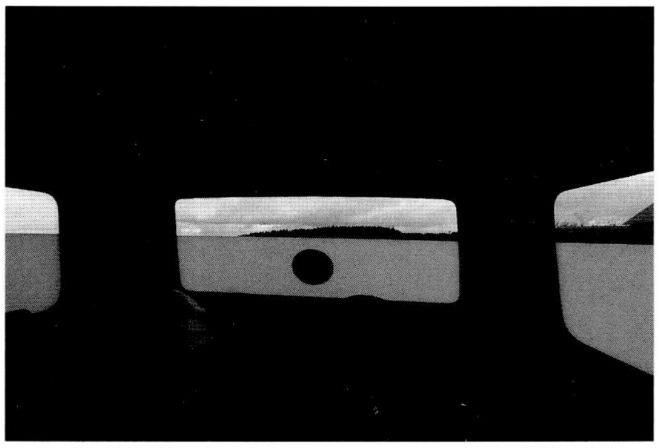

Self portrait – "After the car crash", 1991.
In hospital just after I learned
that my husband had not survived the
accident.

"Light in the distance", 1991.
In the ambulance while being
transported from a small hospital
at the Czech border to Munich.

ness, is of far greater importance to a devastated heart". Van Gogh replied that if a painter has not suffered, he has nothing to paint; happiness deadened the senses, the artist needed suffering as his nourishment. I, too, believe that too much happiness can muddy the goal of life.

Prawns, in order to grow, have to keep shedding their former shell. It may be painful, but it is the only way for them to develop and flourish. I hope that in my artistic development I have made at least some small progress of this kind. In 1997 and 1998, two exhibitions were held entitled *Associations with Death*. In my way I was trying to "digest" my experience of death. I sometimes wish I were a wholly happy person; but everything needs time, everything has its expiry date. The pendulum sometimes has a very long way to travel.

If I were not an artist and able to communicate my experiences and to let others share them, I might never have recovered my energy and joy in life. In 1994, I made a short black-and-white film called *Broken Moon*. My working title was simply "Dreams".

A Chinese woman, unable to sleep, drifts around at night like a somnambulist, alone and aimless, through a — for her — unfamiliar Western metropolis. She comes across dream-like situations that unfold symbolic or metaphorical meanings. Certain incidents elicit a mood of yearning; others are less pleasant, even repellent. She walks past a lot windows in which she sees images of birth, death and love, life's most important stations, to which I devote much space in my creative work. Confused, she stands at a road junction, not knowing which way to turn. Another scene takes place in a bar, where some people are apathetic and bored, others restless. Naked men and women, touching physically, are prevented from recognizing each other, because they are wearing masks. Relationships like this both estrange and alarm the somnambulist. In her idealistic view of things, a relationship is only possible when both bodily and spiritual union occur. She flees from the city to woods, hoping to escape these spectres, but they turn up there as well. In the end she comes to a lake that is frozen over except for a hole in the middle. She reaches out for the moon reflected in the water, but realizes she cannot grasp the moon, only a broken chimera.

In Chinese imagery the full moon is a symbol of perfection. The film attempts to ask whether perfection has any reality in the world, a question I was asking myself at the time. Perfection may be no more than an illusion; like the moon, it can be glimpsed but not grasped. All we can catch of it is a reflection, a phantom. Still, I would like to hang onto my dreams.

The film also bears on freedom. Because of my personal history, it is what I value above all else, even today. It is why, as in the past, I keep returning to Germany even though China has a lot more to offer in many ways, and materially speaking things would be better for me there than in Europe.

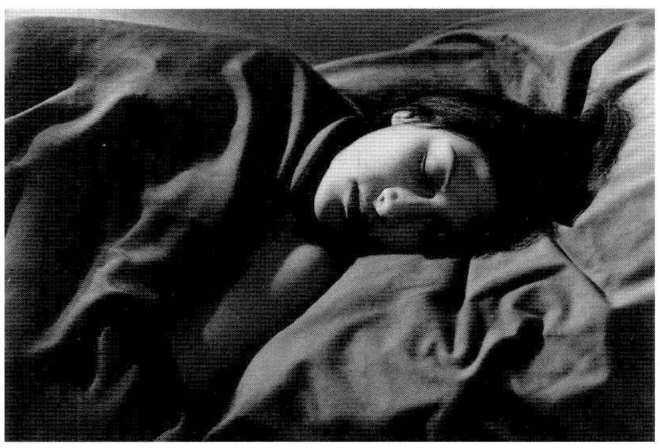

The dream sequence in *The Broken Moon.*

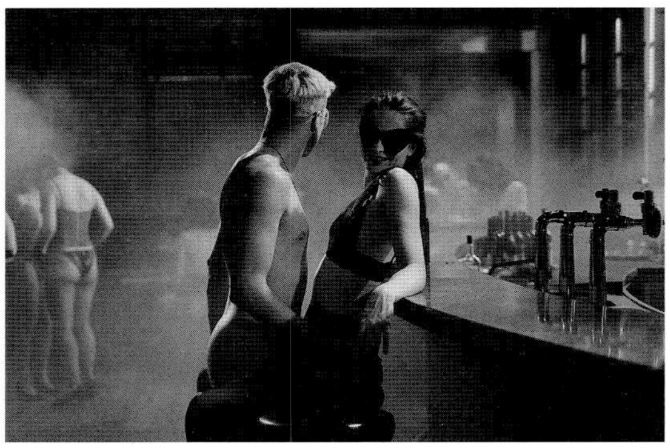

The bar scene from the film *The Broken Moon.*

Freedom, someone once said, is like a ladder, one must only climb up it. Life is not so different. Not everything you want is easy to have.

Before coming to Germany, I was well situated in China. I had a good job at a famous university. I had also had the good fortune to be able to do a three-year extension course to work on a doctoral thesis. Statistics published around the time of the 1995 World Congress for Women showed that no more than a little over a thousand women had been privileged to take such a course up till then. As a young architect, I had already led building projects in China, something that can take years in the West. In these ways, I had made a small name for myself.

Abroad, however, I was unknown and knew no one. In every sphere of life I had to make a fresh start. Yet this was the only way to freedom. On the other hand, I was able to choose my career and its scope, and I could shape my own lifestyle freely. This would have been quite unthinkable in China only fifteen years earlier.

How can a traditional Chinese woman run fast when her feet have been bound since she was small? She must first learn to walk normally before trying to take bigger strides. For years I yearned for a freer life. The external conditions for a different life were now there in my new Western world, but it took me a long time to get used to them. I thought, with my flexibility and my capacity for grasping things quickly, that the process would be swift. But then I saw that liberation takes much longer.

In 1987, I wrote an article for the book *China and Women*, which was published in Germany. I said there that although I was an architect I wished to devote my life to photography, writing and film-making, and I quoted a Chinese proverb: "When the cart reaches the mountain, a path will appear". I had made this my own life principle.

Ten years later, a German women's magazine dug up the subject again and republished my old article. They wanted to demonstrate how wishes can be nurtured, for in the meantime mine had all come true.

Lin's death brought life's fragility home to me – how it can all be over in a second. From now on I wanted to live every moment consciously. Whether it was work, free-time or pleasure, my attitude to time changed. I sought concentrated experience. My work used to be extremely goal-oriented; today, the work itself, as a creative process, is central. It gives my life meaning, pleasure and joy. It also enables me to make my contribution for others. I would like to be able to say, before I die, that my life has been worthwhile. I consistently followed the path of becoming an artist.

Naturally, the recognition my work receives and the social success connected with it are important incentives as well. Project followed hard upon project, I was permanently occupied. Some of my friends suspected I was becoming a workaholic to escape from loneliness. I am not sure, however, that they are right.

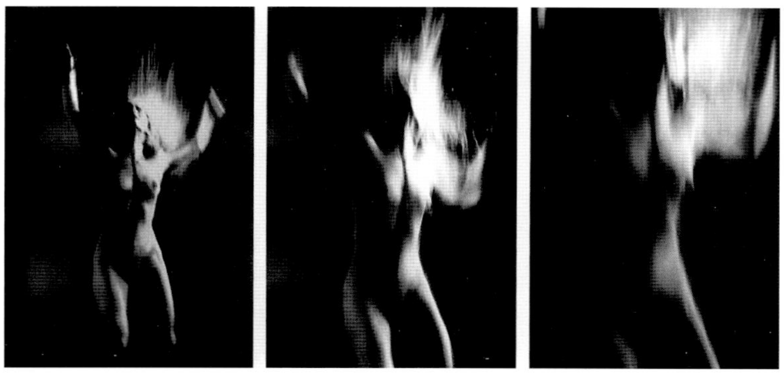

"Selfextrication
No. 8, 9, 10", 1992

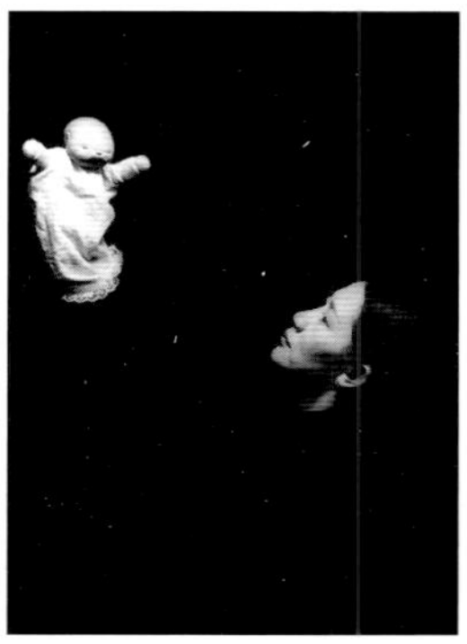

Self portrait –
"Dream of my own child,
No. 3", 1996

Since childhood I have had no proper home. I moved to Shanghai at the age of nineteen and lived for many years in a student hostel. Lin and I planned to have a child and to set up a real home once we had been allowed to reside permanently in Germany. His sudden death put an end to that. My parents once told me they owed their life to their child. For, without this child, they would never have survived the terrible era of the Cultural Revolution.

In summer 1996, a pianist friend of mine, Monika Leonhard, invited me to a chamber music festival she was organizing near Naples. I despaired of ever experiencing anything like cheerfulness again. But then in these surroundings in the south of Italy, it was as if I had woken up after long hibernation. There I was, under the southern sun; the warmth of the people, their different manners, their cheerfulness and easygoing lifestyle, all appealed to me. I could not help but ask the reason for such striking qualities, and was told that living near a volcano, which from earliest times had cost many lives, alters one's attitude to life, because every day may be the last. Why under such circumstances should one not enjoy each day? One of my own nude photos came to mind, of a man with a big mirror on his back. His burden is evident. I called the picture "heavy personal load". It also depicted my own oppressive situation. Liberation is not only a question of external chains, but of mental bonds as well. Why had I been chasing things I could not have, instead of appreciating what I had? The complete freedom I had acquired, for instance, and which many doubtless envied me for. These experiences and my new-found happiness re-awoke a desire to travel, which I did, far and frequently.

To judge by my flight schedule I might be an air hostess. The past five years have seen me travelling far more often than I have been at home, and my Munich flat is more like a hotel room than anything else. My father drew a picture of me, suitcase in hand, key round my neck. My household. He forgot my camera and diary. The portraits in this book are a small portion of my photographs taken while travelling. On my birthday a friend lip-sticked a red balloon in my guestbook, string attached to a Munich rooftop, and wrote: "It's great to have you with us again in Munich". Other friends compare me to the wind. You can see a balloon, but the wind just comes and goes, leaving no trace. My wanderlust, my yearning to go out and meet "the other", also has to do with the fact that in China for almost thirty years I could not travel abroad. I still love being able to travel as much as and wherever I want.

My trips vary enormously and are often not precisely planned. I am a traveller, not a tourist. What interests me are not so much sights but the mood of a place and all the various chance occurrences. My senses are completely open then, and there are always so many marvellous things waiting to be discovered.

One of the calligraphic works in my flat is a proverb by Lao-tzu. Friends, who can read it, call it highly ironical. He says that the further one travels, the less one understands, and that while a saint

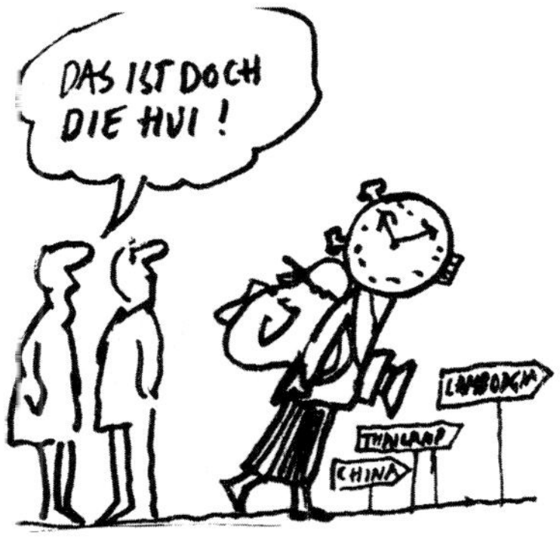

"That's Hui, isn't it?" A cartoon in a German magazine about my life travelling.

Part of the series: "Flower Souls", 2000

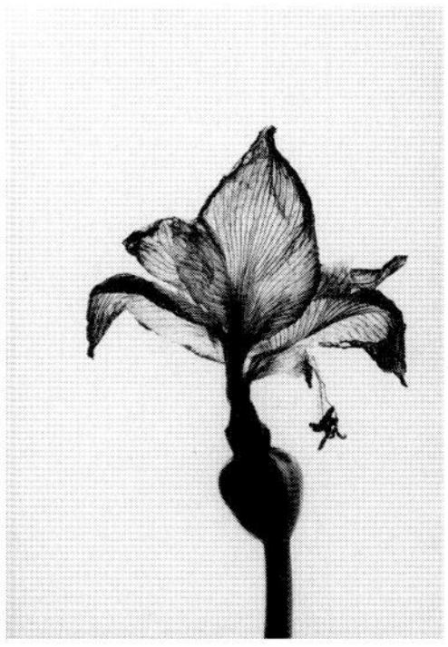

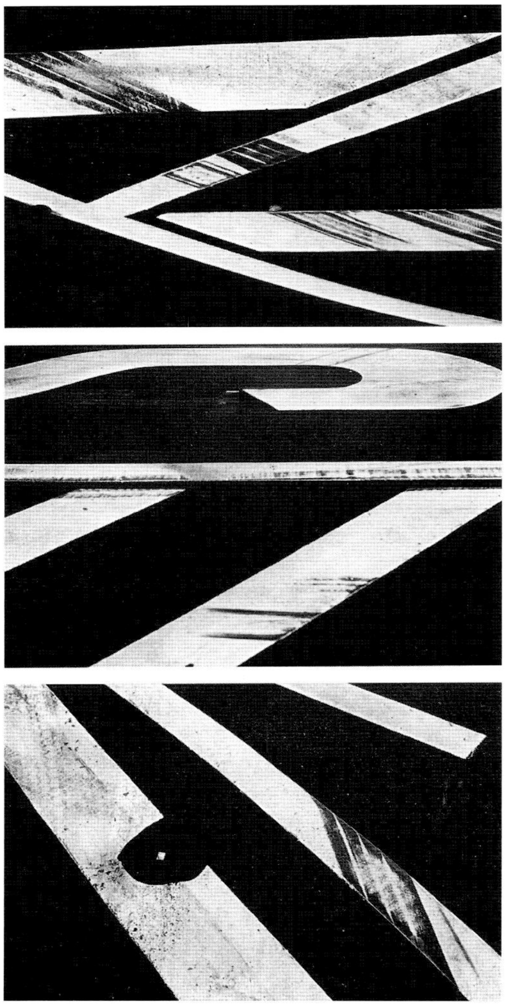

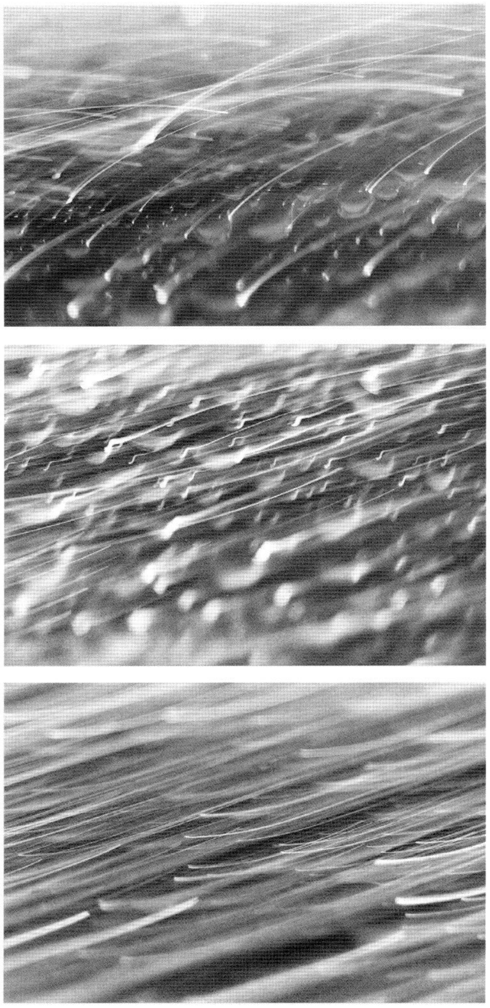

Untitled, 1990

Untitled, 2001

never travels, he understands the whole world. I think he wanted to say we should spend more time in peaceful contemplation than in perpetual action. Another of his proverbs says, "It is better to go ten thousand miles than to read ten thousand books". That is closer to me. At home things tend to be hectic rather than otherwise. Travelling is when I manage to relax. It is the time for new input, the time for reflection as well. My travel notes have a different quality to those I write at home. It is as if spatial distance were a source of intellectual and spiritual inspiration.

I am one of those people who draw deeply on the past. Every moment experienced is tomorrow's past. It, too, will pass and be forgotten. My mother often regrets not having lived more consciously. Unlike me, she could not record the moments of her life with camera 67and diary.

I used to photograph mainly cities and landscapes. Three travel books in the *Seeing and Experiencing* series were the result, and I think they summarize my travels very well. Some people travel better without a camera. They can take in their new impressions more easily that way. For me the opposite is true. My camera helps me see and experience the world more intensely. Otherwise I would forget what I experience much more quickly. People's faces have always fascinated me far more than architecture and landscapes ever could. Photography has become a way of life, a part of my daily existence. Whether as a form of artistic expression or, more journalistically, as a record of things chiefly of personal importance, I cannot imagine living without it. My love for photography is so great that it has become a regular obsession.

Over the past two years, flowers have exerted a constant fascination on me. I have frequently found myself circling one at night, camera in hand, photographing it from innumerable angles. I call myself a photographer only reluctantly, for like all such professional labels it tends to enjoin a certain monotony of practice. This detracts from the spontaneous act and diminishes photography's attractiveness in my eyes.

Unexpectedly, while travelling, I found myself coming back to abstract photography again, which had been one of my central interests when I was first in Europe. Colour, form and composition play a big role here. That I returned to colour photography after a long black-and-white phase, addressing themes such as the emotions and human relationships, had to do with a basic change in underlying mood.

My photography has two major strands, the one independent and autonomous, the other closer to documentary photography. Deliberate artistic creation necessitates a theme, a plan, just as a film needs a script. In my projects on yin and yang, or on self-liberation, good planning was an essential part of success. Setting, lighting, appropriate models, were all indispensable. My other photographic direction, however, involves chance, spontaneity, unplanned events. This

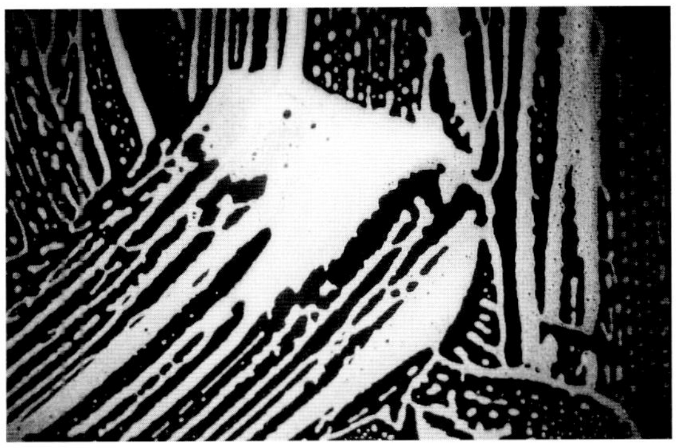

Untitled, 1999

Part of the series:
"Flower Souls", 2000

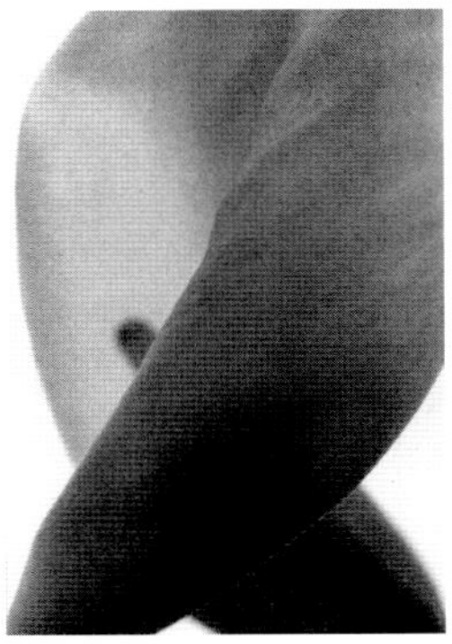

could create the erroneous impression that I work without any plan at all. Documentary films, which do stake a certain claim to be art, are comparable here. Indeed, they sometimes presuppose even greater skill, as it is not generally possible to repeat a process.

Human beauty or ugliness are unimportant when I take photographs. What in life is ugly can be beautiful in art. My chief criterion is truth, the honest rendition of what I have seen. I avoid the smiling poses people often adopt in front of the camera just to please. I favour natural lighting and seldom use flash. A straightforward picture lets situation and expression of eyes speak for themselves. Traditional Chinese thinking says it is impolite to look a stranger in the eyes. I do look at people directly, however, if a face appeals to me, especially when I am travelling in a new place. And people are often surprized that I look at them so directly, until I explain I just want to take a photo. Eyes fascinate me. They are the most expressive part of the human body, and I am often amazed how extraordinarily beautiful the eyes of quite "ordinary" people can be. I try to speak with each subject. I go up very close. That used to be unthinkable for me. I wanted to stop using the telephoto altogether and photograph my subjects with only a standard lens. It was not easy to begin with.

In a book about my portrait photographs, the Chinese critic Lin Lu wrote: "All of her subjects face the camera directly, and although none of the encounters is rehearsed, when a shot is taken, photographer and subject stand in a natural relation. Xiao Hui Wang has laid aside big lenses in favour of eye-to-eye dialogue. Such direct exchange gives her access to her subjects' entire inner worlds. The American photographer Mark Chester has said it took him twenty years to abandon the telephoto and stop hiding behind a lens. Xiao Hui Wang turned her back on this sort of thing very quickly, and sought communication instead ...".

The faces in this book often express things that I cannot easily put into words. Candid honesty glows in the Indian boy's eyes; the child's eyes put me in mind of a stream's clear water; the Tibetan farmer's eyes bespeak an independent, heart-warming uprightness; the hundred-year-old man seems timeless; the friend's reticent eyes say more than many words can express; and the girl's friendly smile goes straight to every viewer's heart.

The eyes of the young homeless woman I photographed in Malaga affected me very deeply. The listlessness in them, and apathy, are boundless. I wonder just how much they have experienced. At the time, the story of that old woman came back to me, who "lived for one thing only – to die". I kept thinking of the Malagan woman afterwards. Utterly motionless. She did not even react when I gave her a few coins. Her eyes remained mute.

The life of a travelling woman, changes of address, homelessness, all raise the question of identity. My Publisher, Juergen Tesch, compares home with religion: it is nowhere, yet it remains in the heart. The Chinese are highly aware of their roots. "The leaves fall and

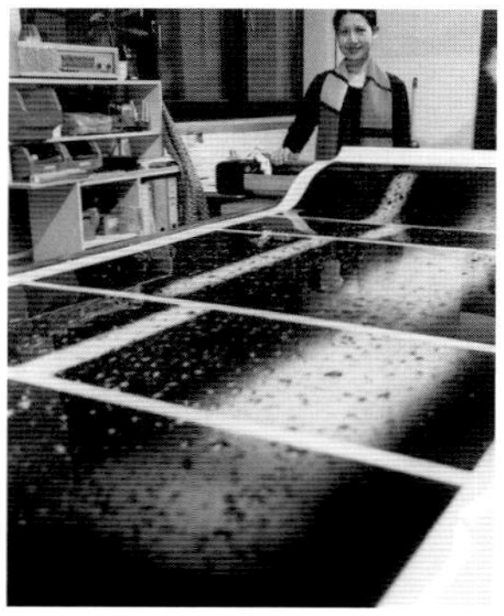

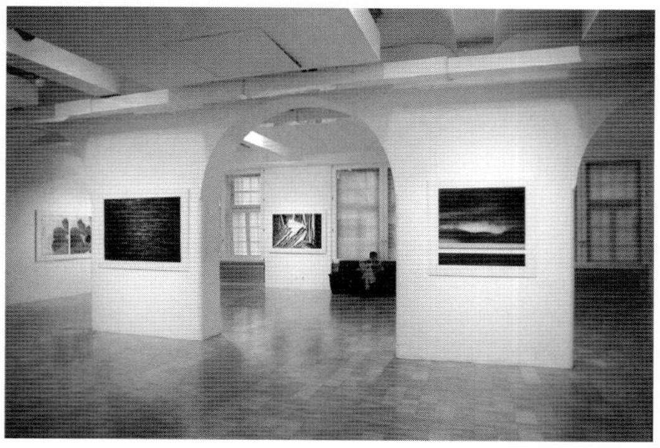

In the photo lab with large-format color photos.

Exhibition of my abstract pictures and flower pictures at the Kunstverein Mannheim, 2001 return to their roots", is a saying. The further one is from home, the stronger the yearning. In my experience it is a basic feeling, but it also comes out in small things such as the slips of red paper bearing the symbol for happiness, which I hang up in my Munich flat at Chinese New Year; I never did in China, finding it tasteless.

For a long time my thoughts circled around the subject of "home". What does it mean? Is it family members, friends, or all the familiar little things? Unfortunately, too many such things are disappearing. I expressed my concern over the irreparable loss of so many traditional things in my documentary film *The Peking Opera Man*, contrasting the life of a performer at the Peking Opera and the increasingly Western-oriented Chinese lifestyle. The film gives expression to my own sadness about the decay of traditional cultural values.

I never used to feel properly at home anywhere. Today, however, I like being everywhere, and that is enough for me. As a Samurai proverb puts it, "A hero is at home throughout the world". Here are some questions I was once asked in an interview and the answers I gave:

Favourite address?	Where I happen to be.
Favourite occupation?	Work creatively.
Forgivable mistake?	Perpetual change.
Greatest misfortune?	Lack of freedom.
Greatest good fortune?	To be able to work creatively.
Most valuable quality?	Imagination.
Favourite condition?	Things passionately begun.
Life philosophy?	"When the cart reaches the mountain, a path will appear".

A fortune-teller in China once predicted a stony path for me until I reached forty, a period of difficulties and suffering. After that he foresaw better times. Today I can say I feel happier almost than I have ever done before, having found the lifestyle that I really enjoy. The main thing is that I am able spontaneously to turn all my thoughts and creativity into art, whether in writing books, or in photography and film. All my energy is able to flow into what I believe I can do best. Considered as a whole, it is a completely natural process.

I sometimes wonder whether each new day is one day more in life or whether it is one day less, have we lost or gained a day? I don't believe I regret any of my days gone by. Although I have experienced enough bad things, innerly I still feel very young.

In my *Visual Diary*, I close with the wish that my life be green like a tree, its roots growing ever deeper, while its branches strive upwards …

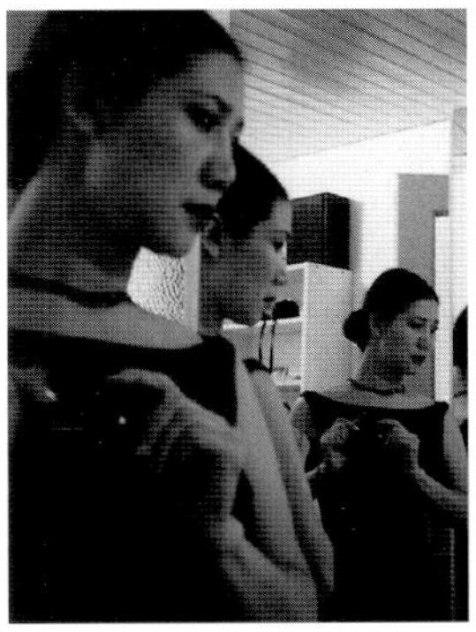

Self-Portrait, 2001

Plates

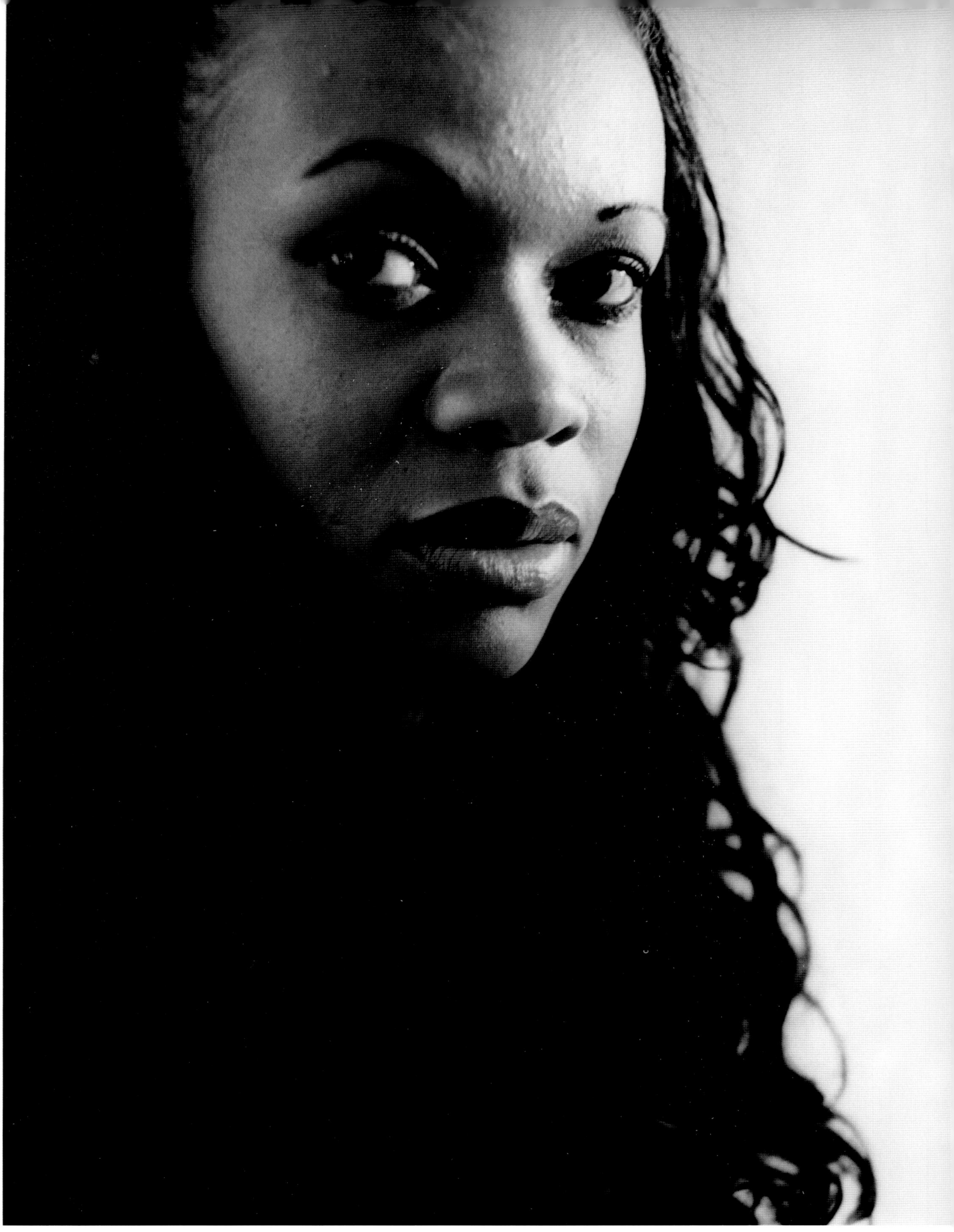

Munich 1997

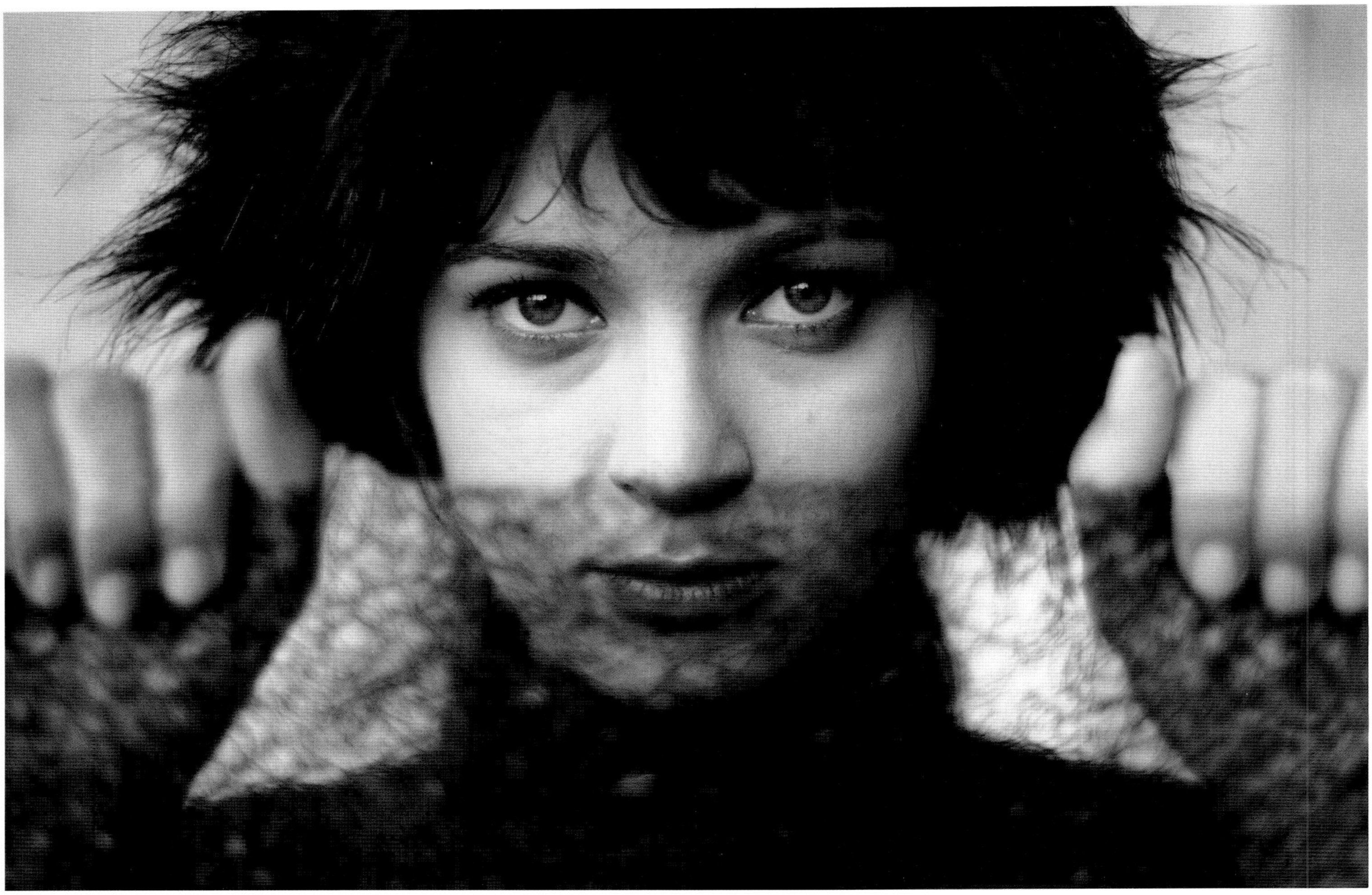

Herten 1999

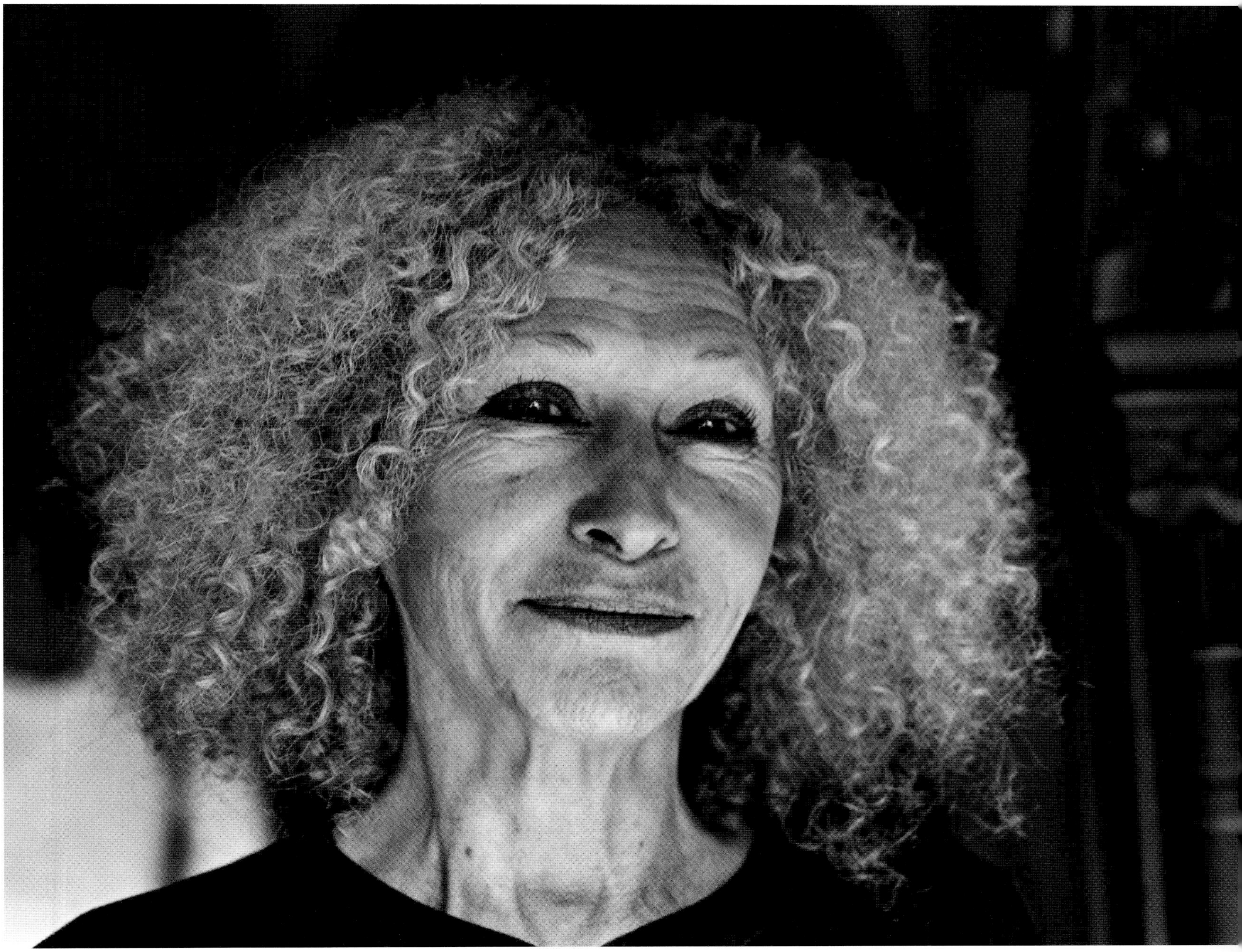

Venice 1998

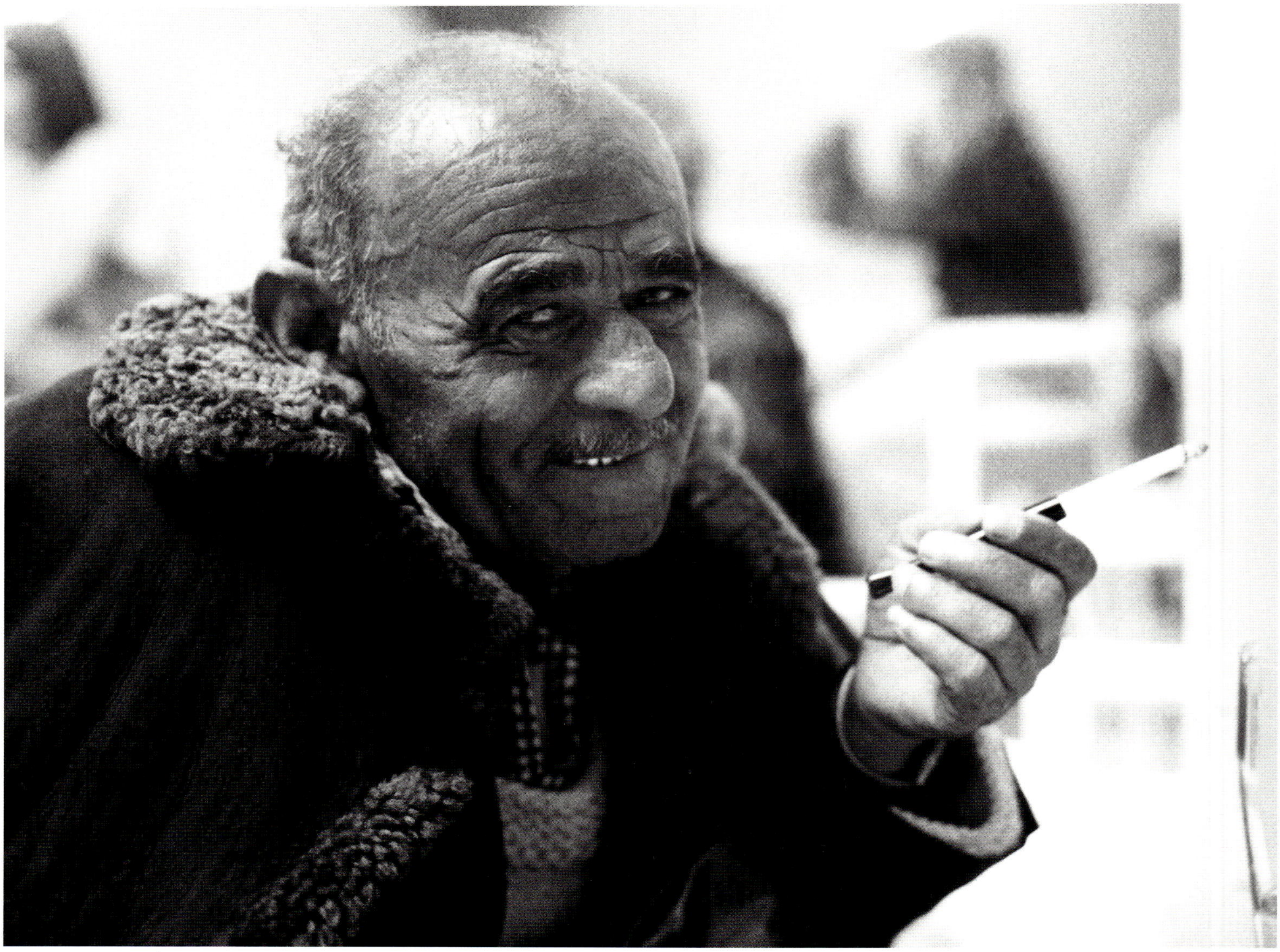

Frankfurt 1991

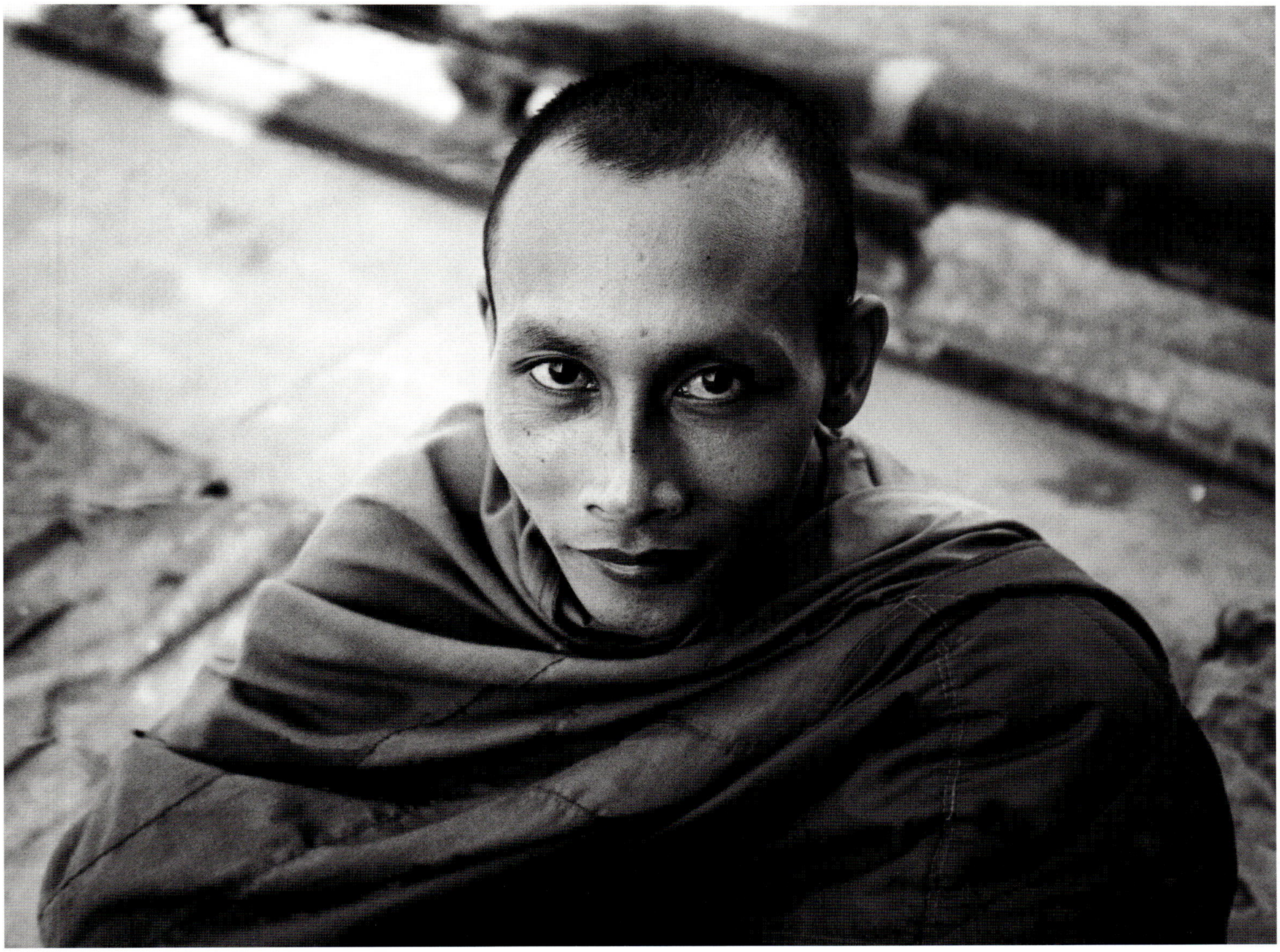

Angkor 2000

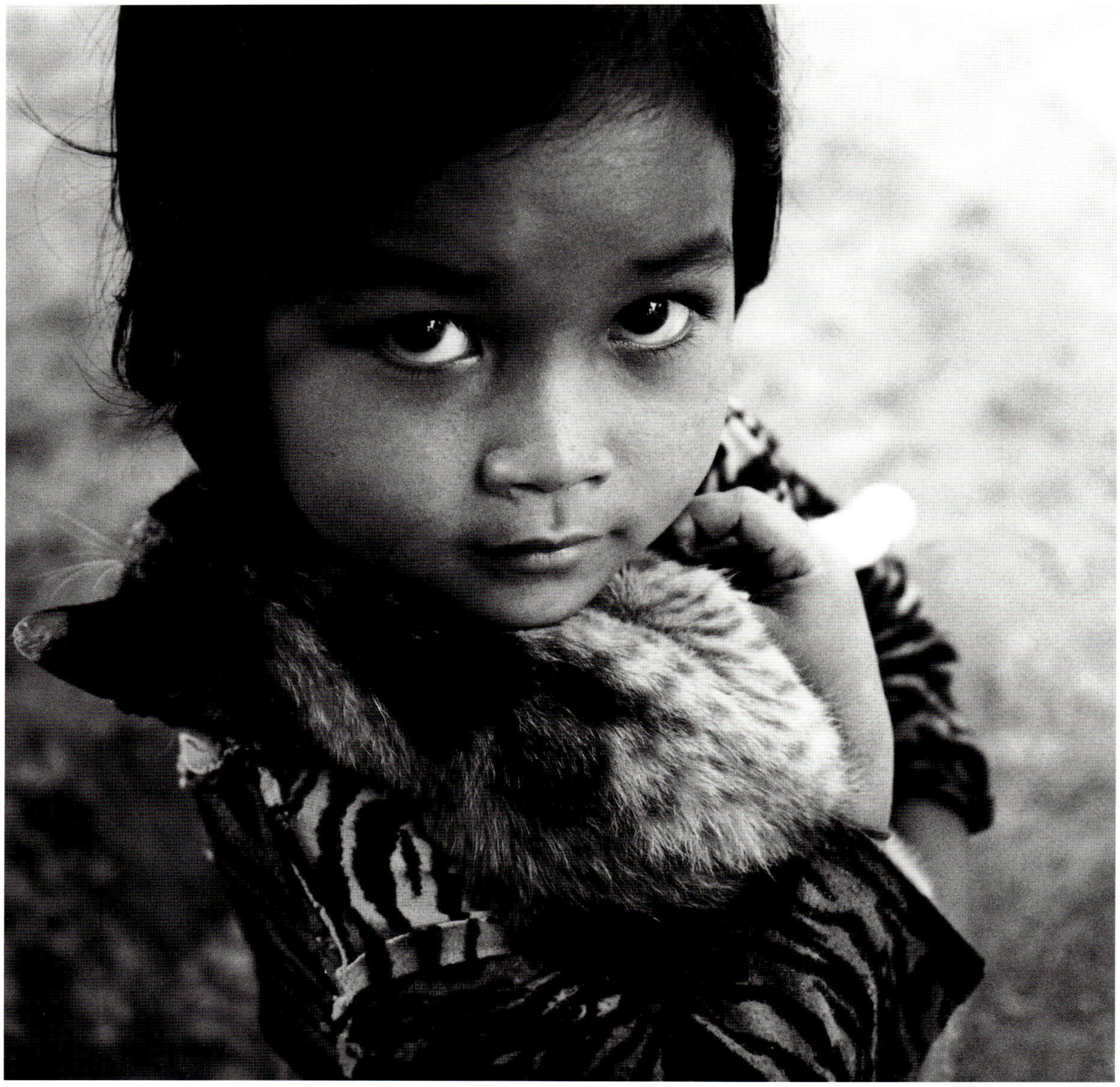

Angkor 2000

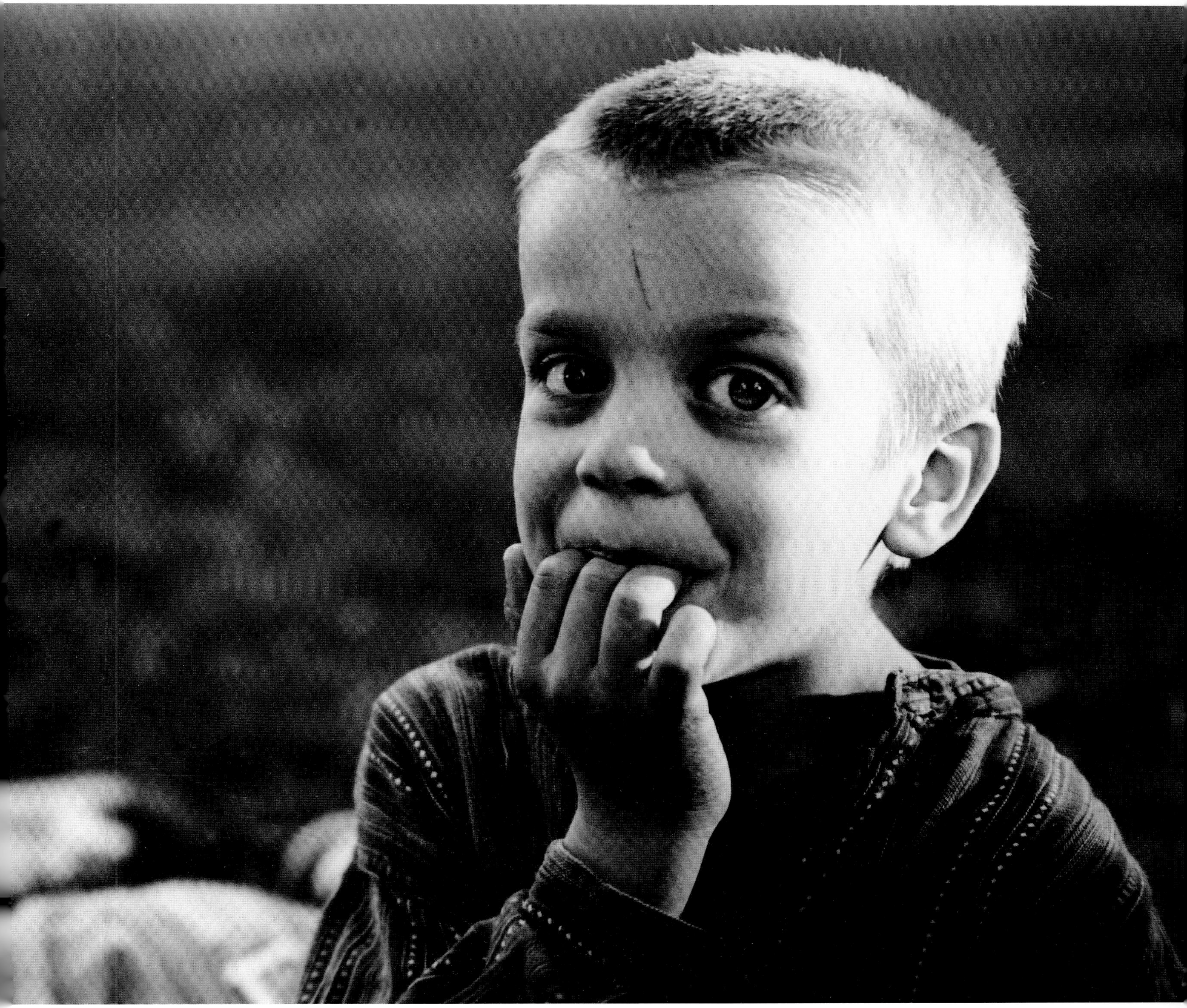

Stockholm 1996

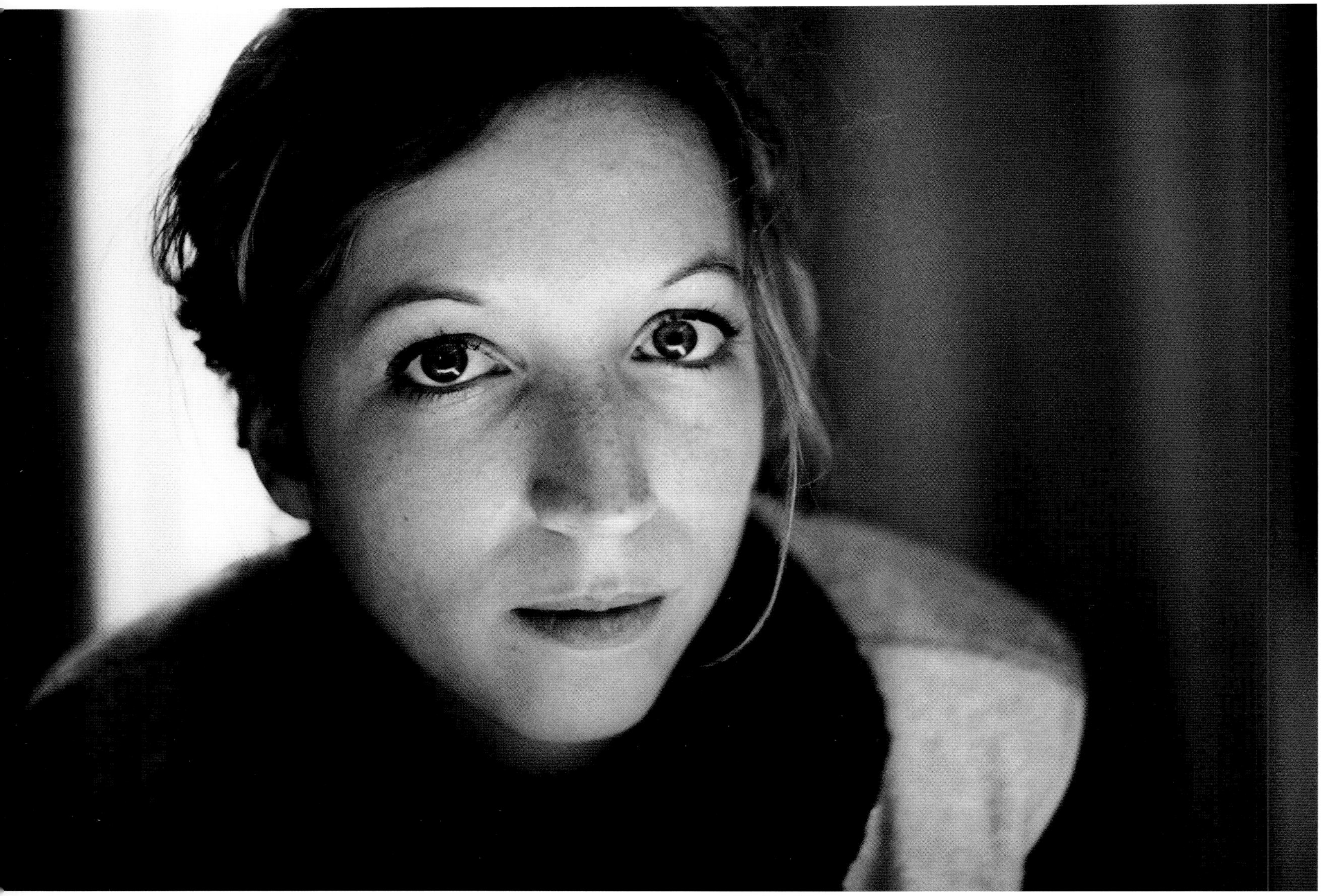

Herten 1999

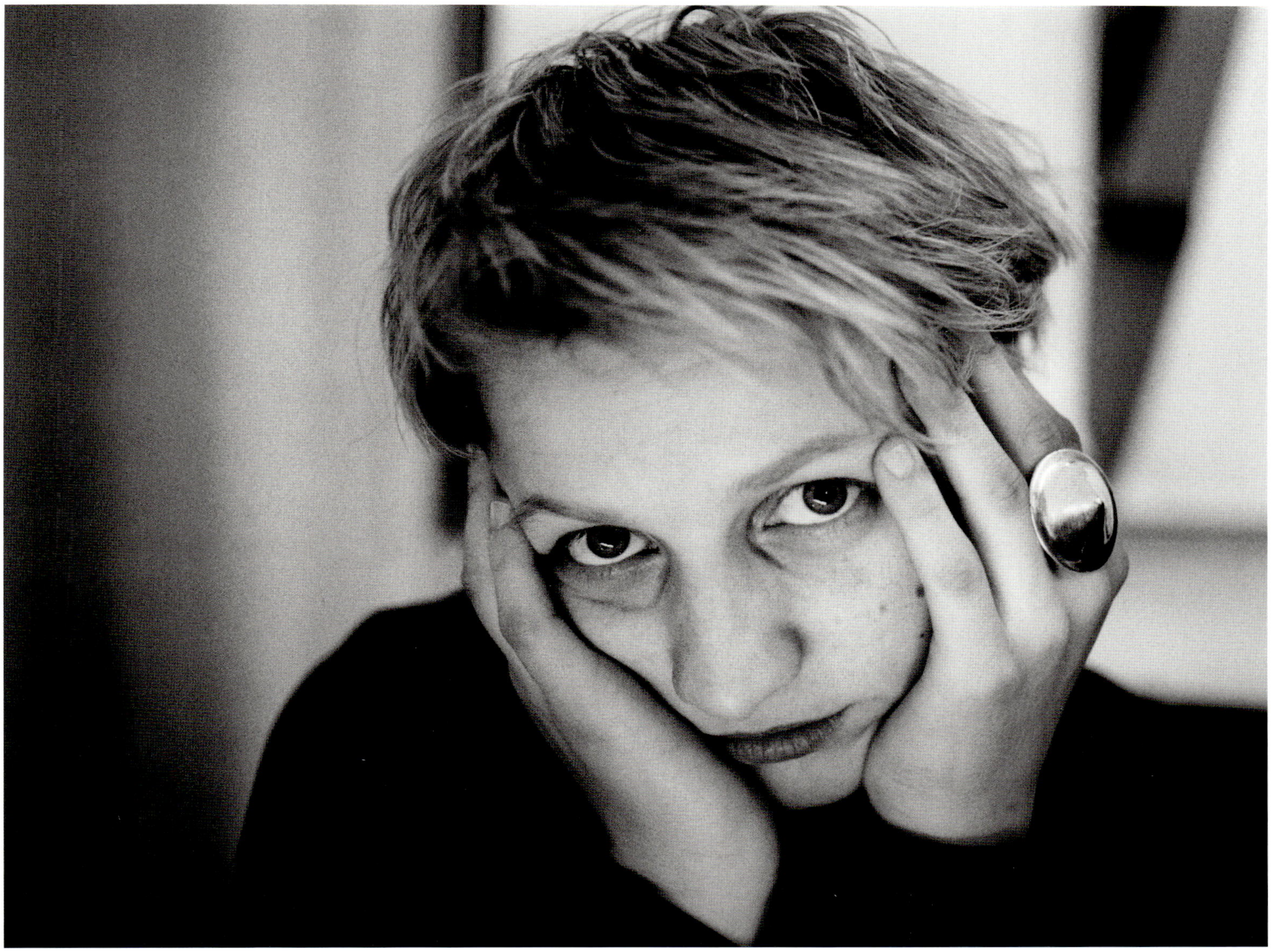

Herter 1999

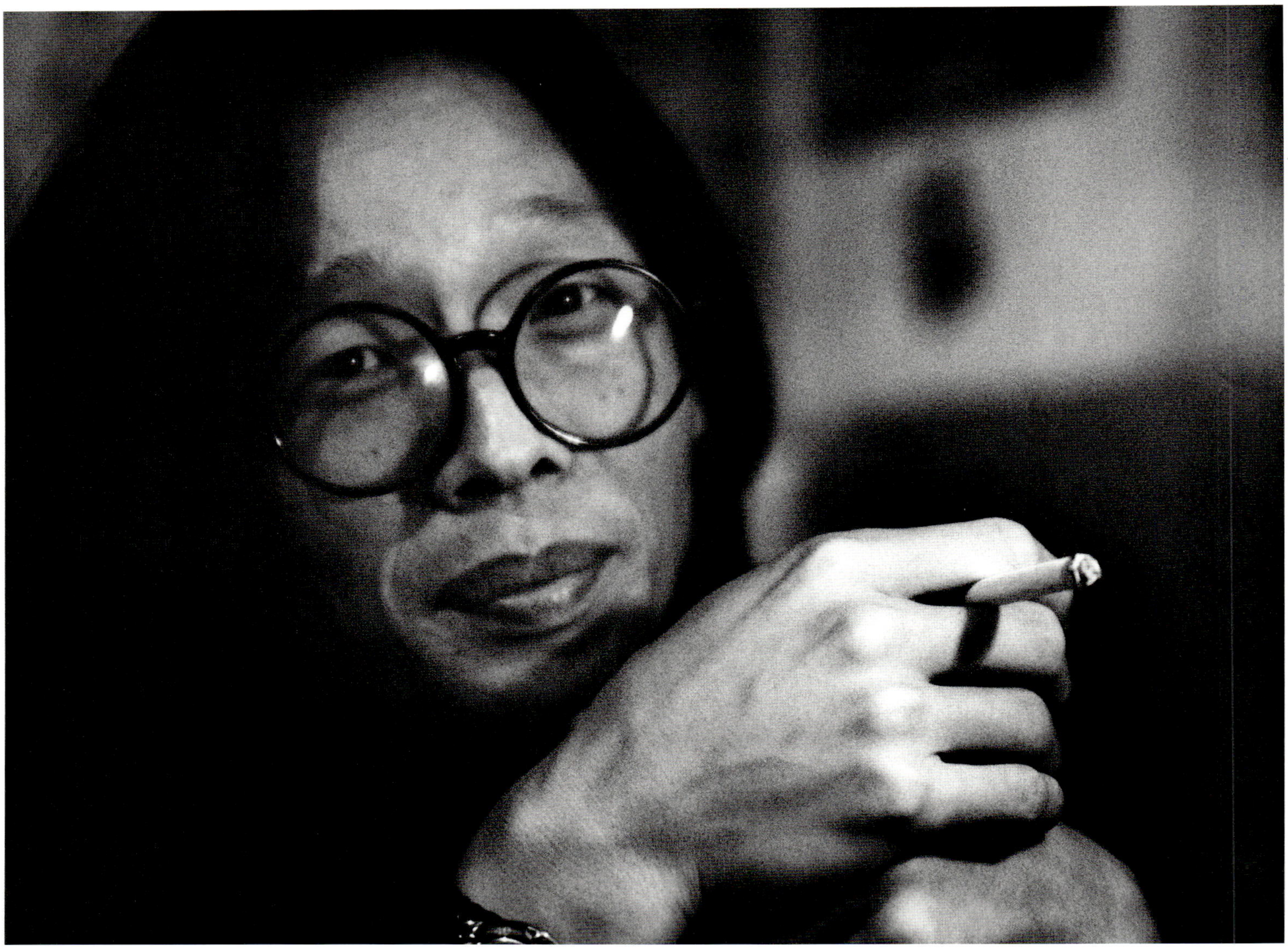

Tianjin 1998

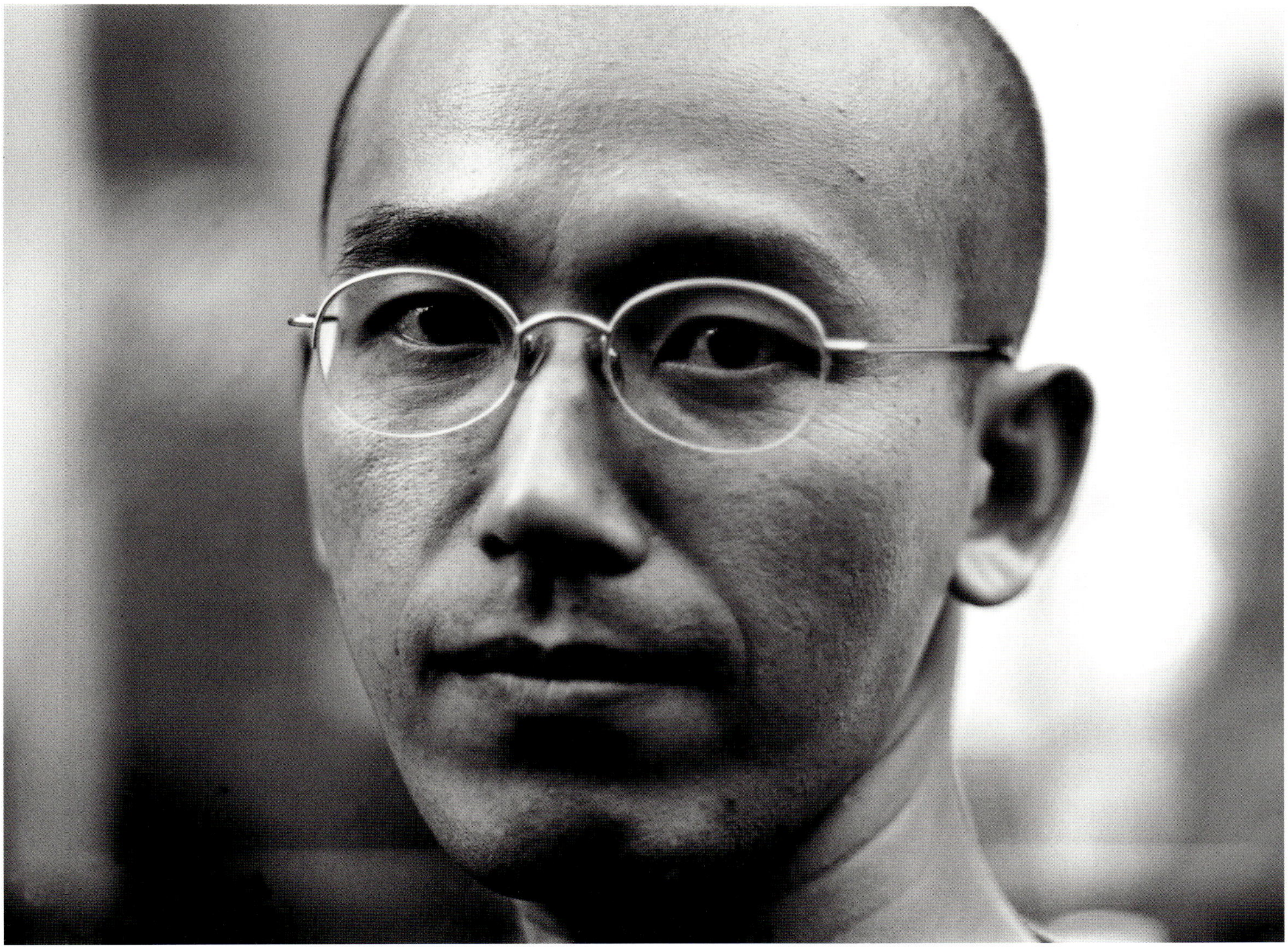

Arles 1999

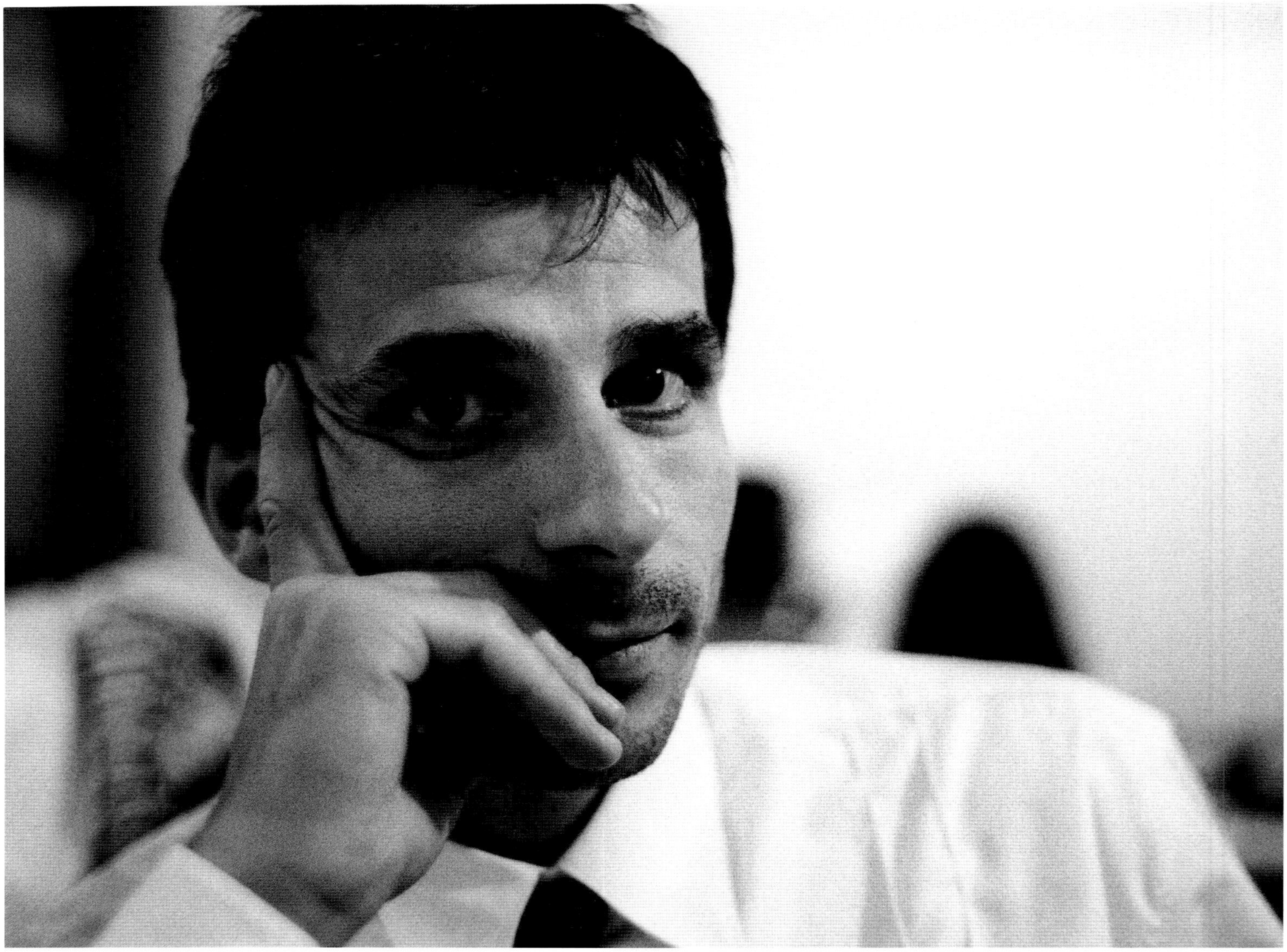

Würzburg 1999

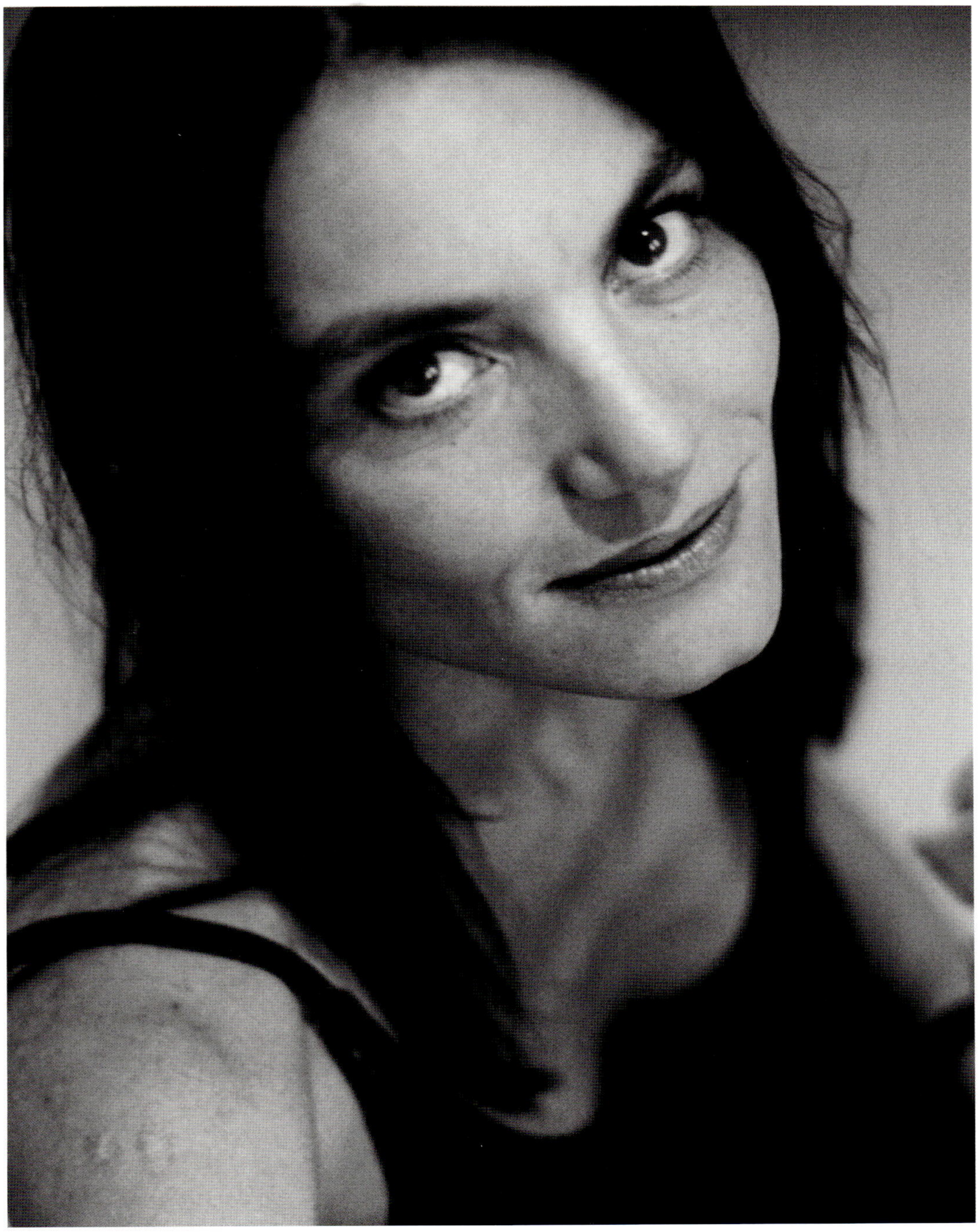

Munich 1999

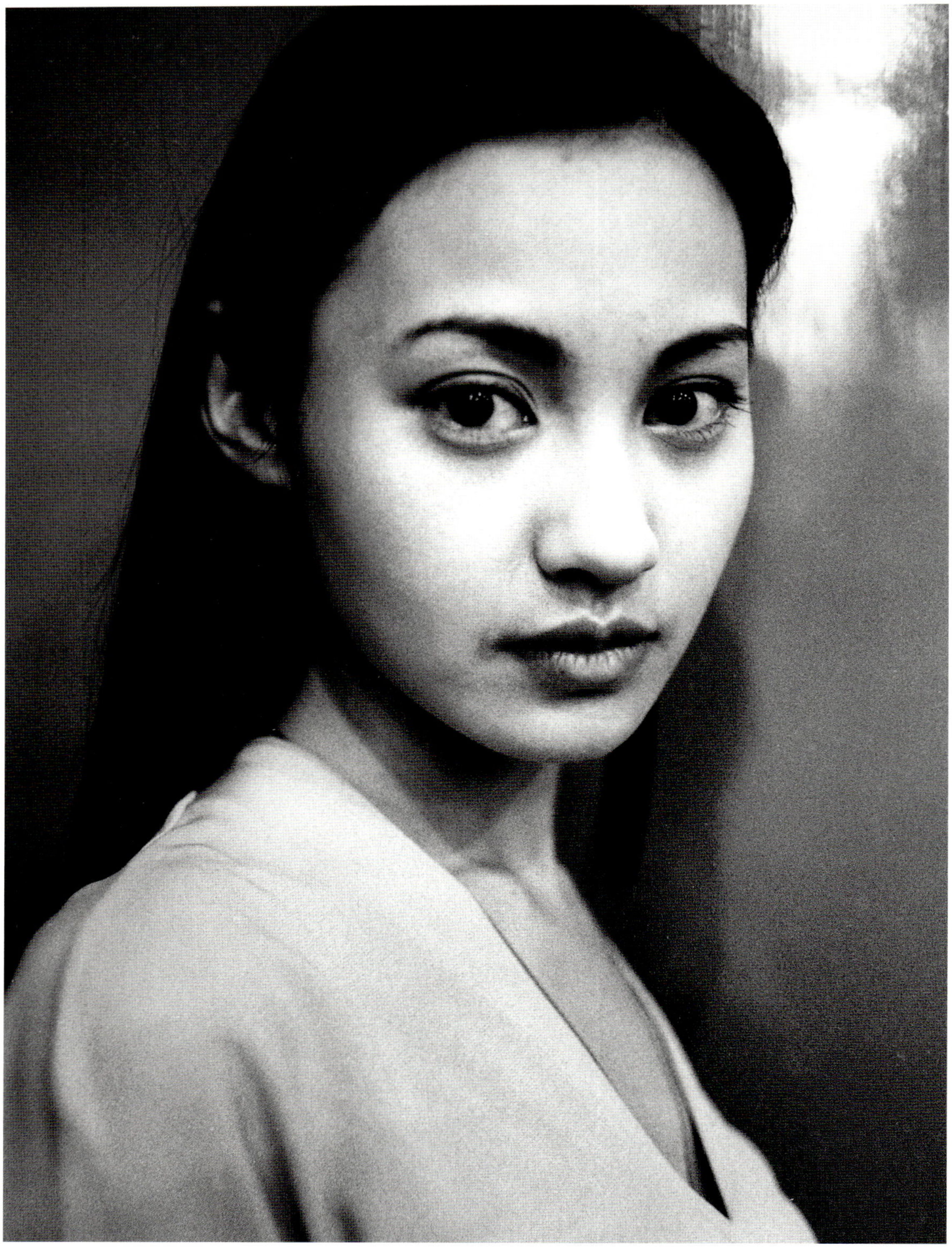

Beijing 2000

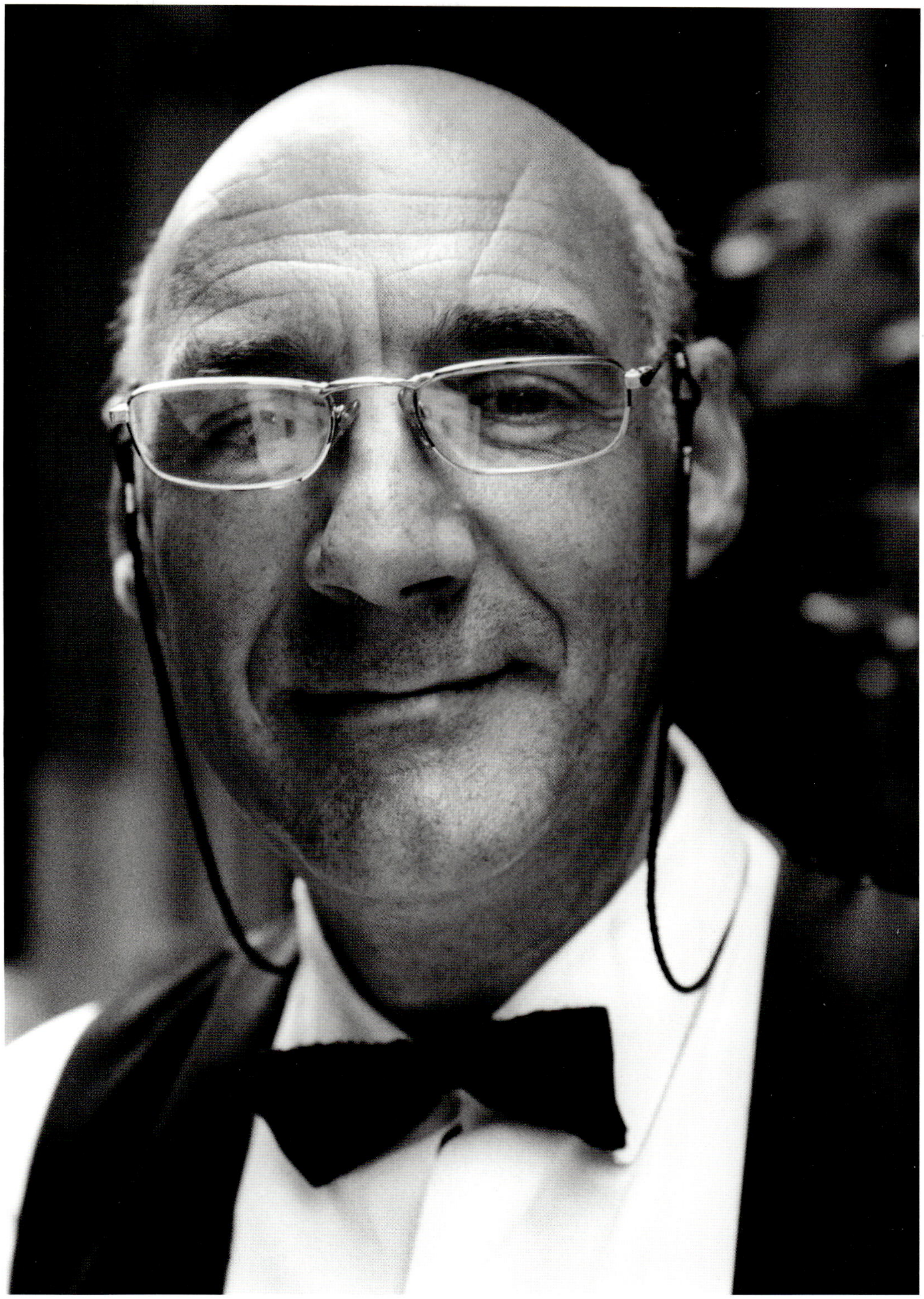

Vienna 1998

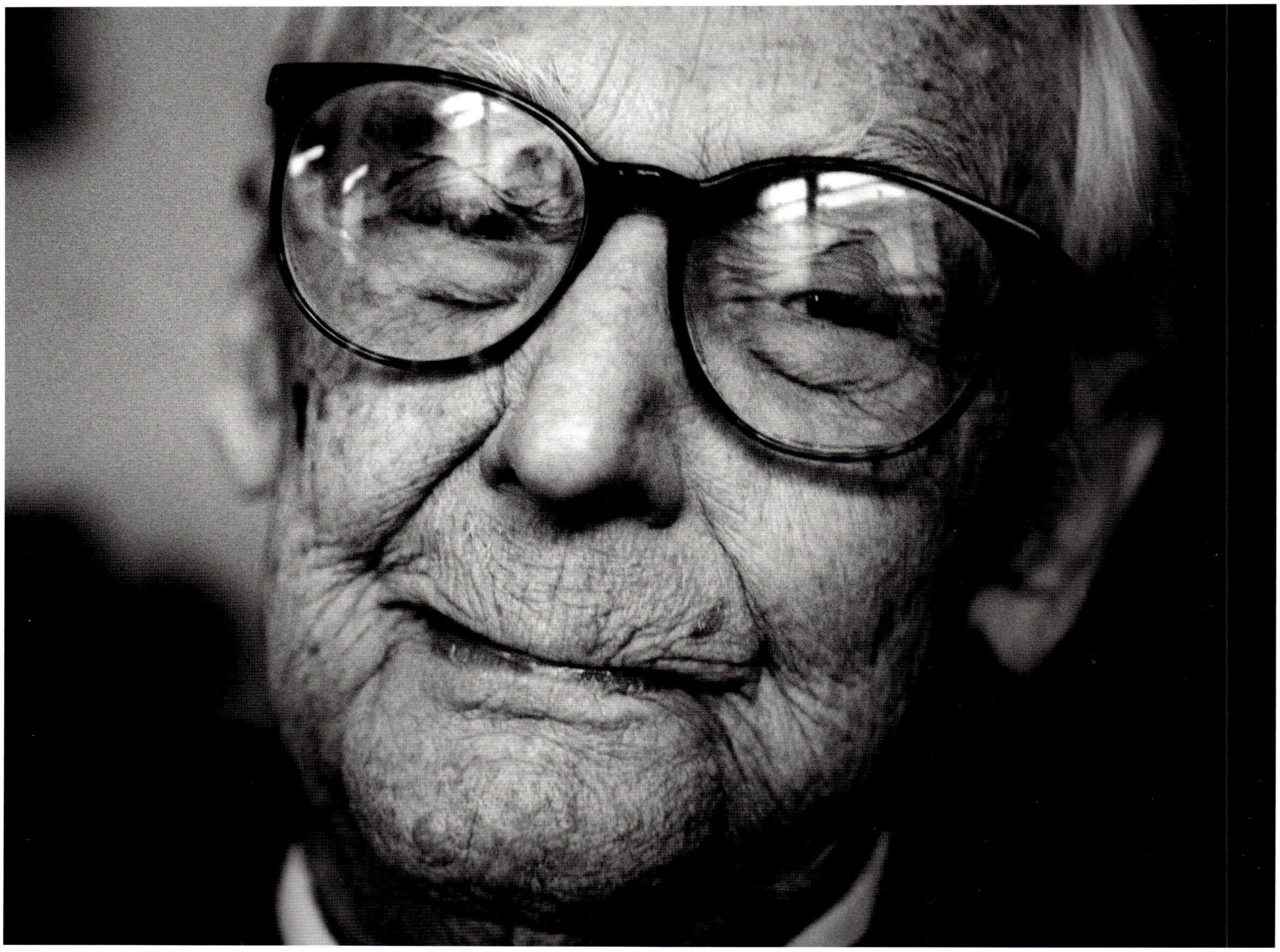

Munich 1999

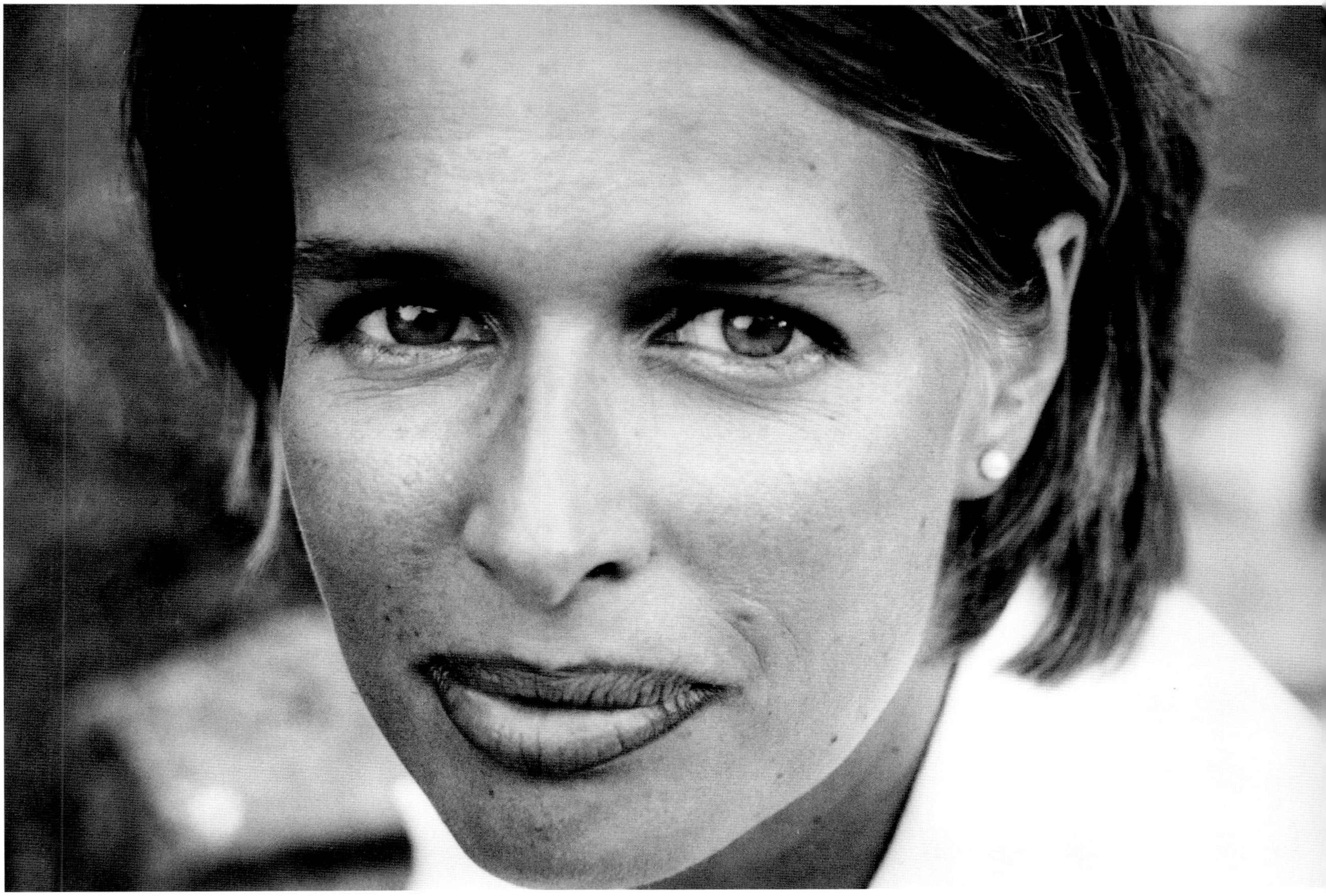

Würzburg 1999

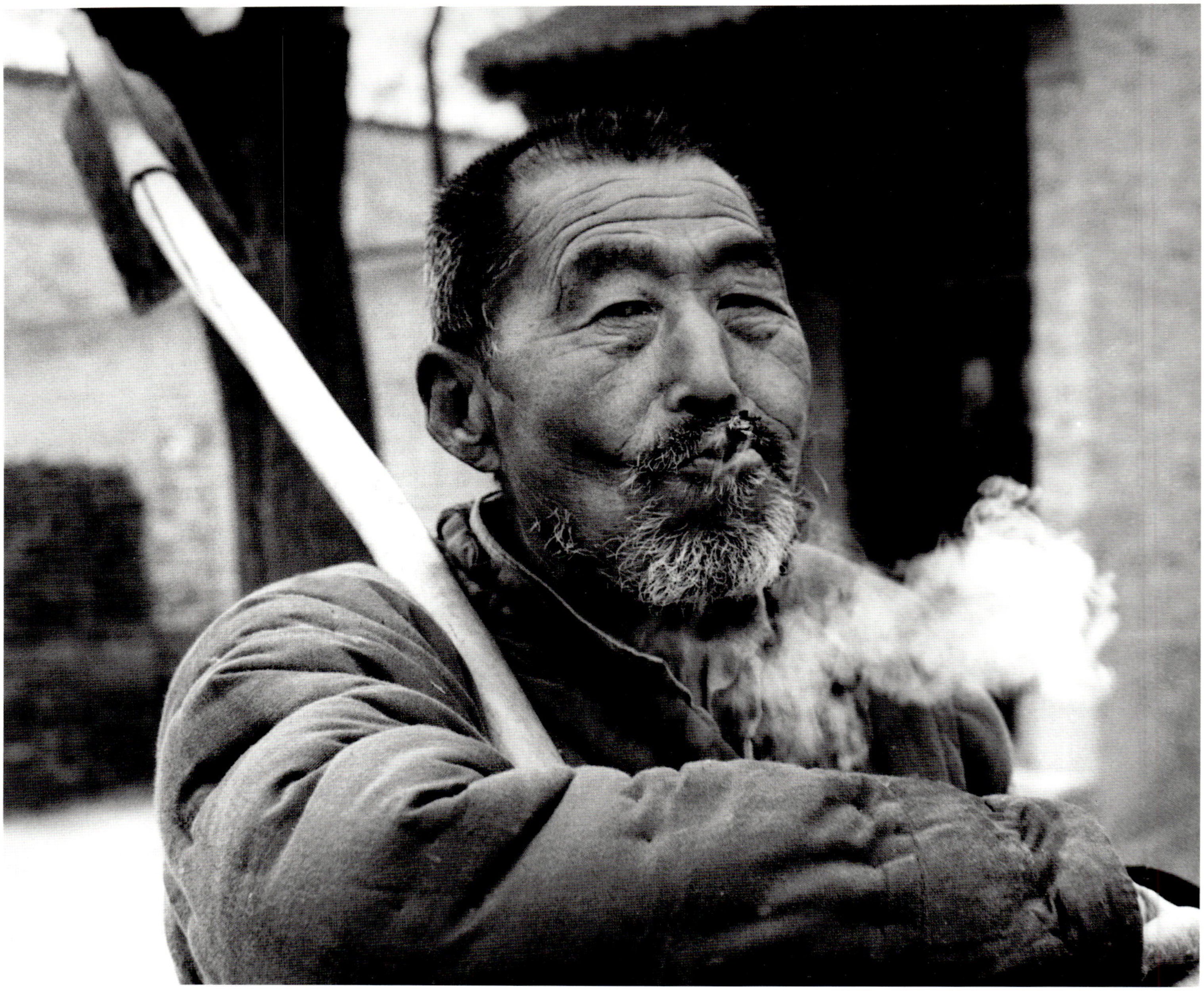

Shanxi 1995

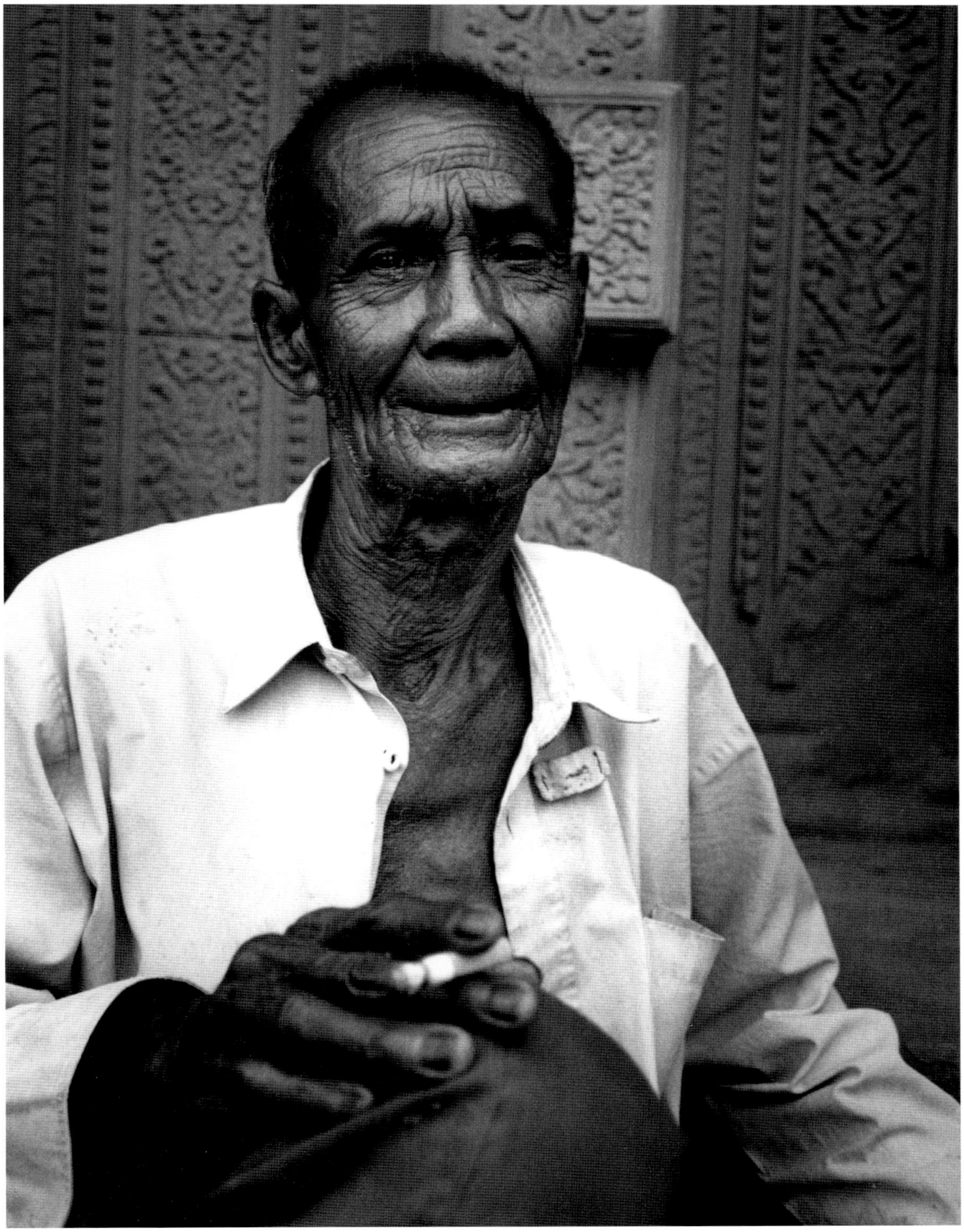

Siem Riap 2000

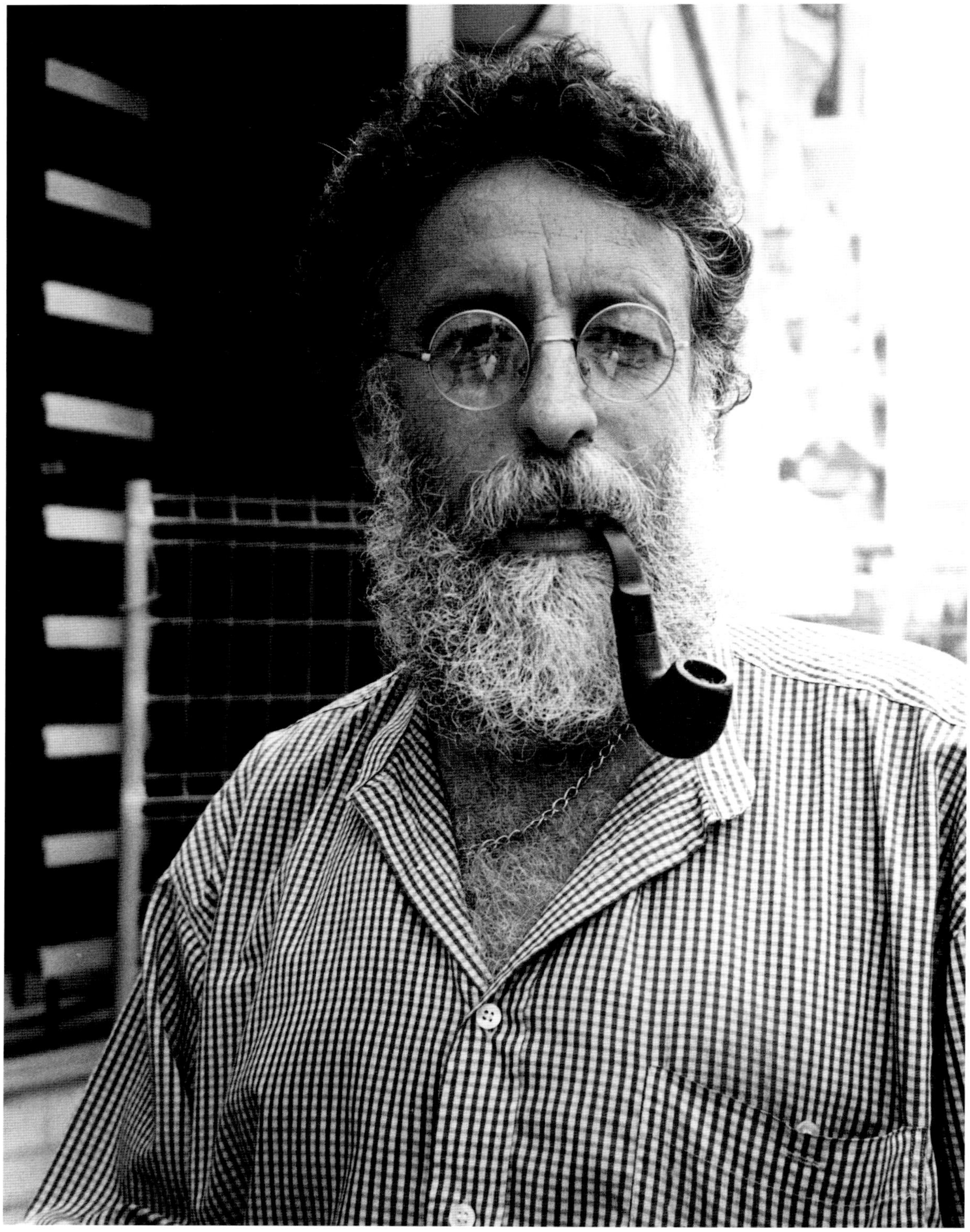

Ronda 1998

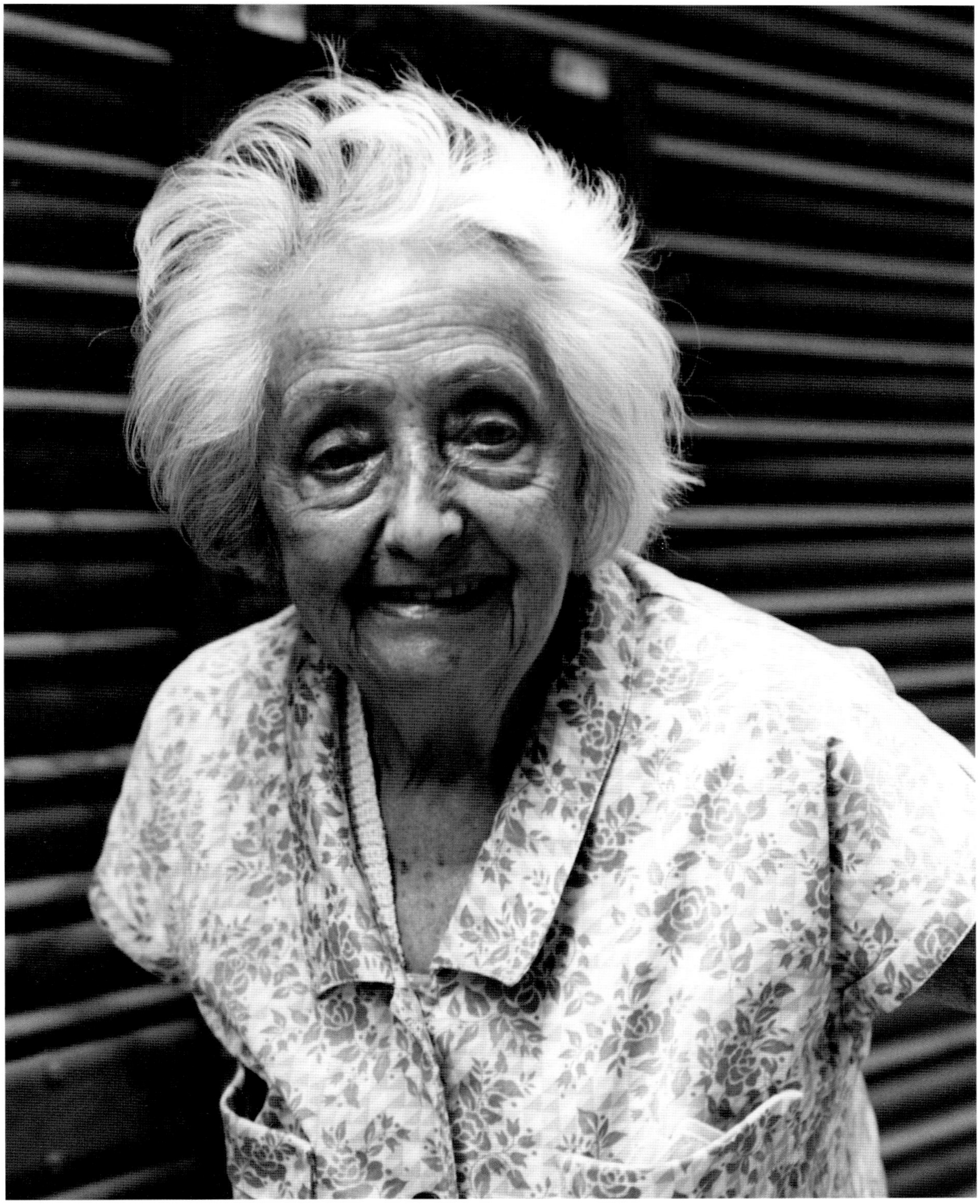

Malaga 1998

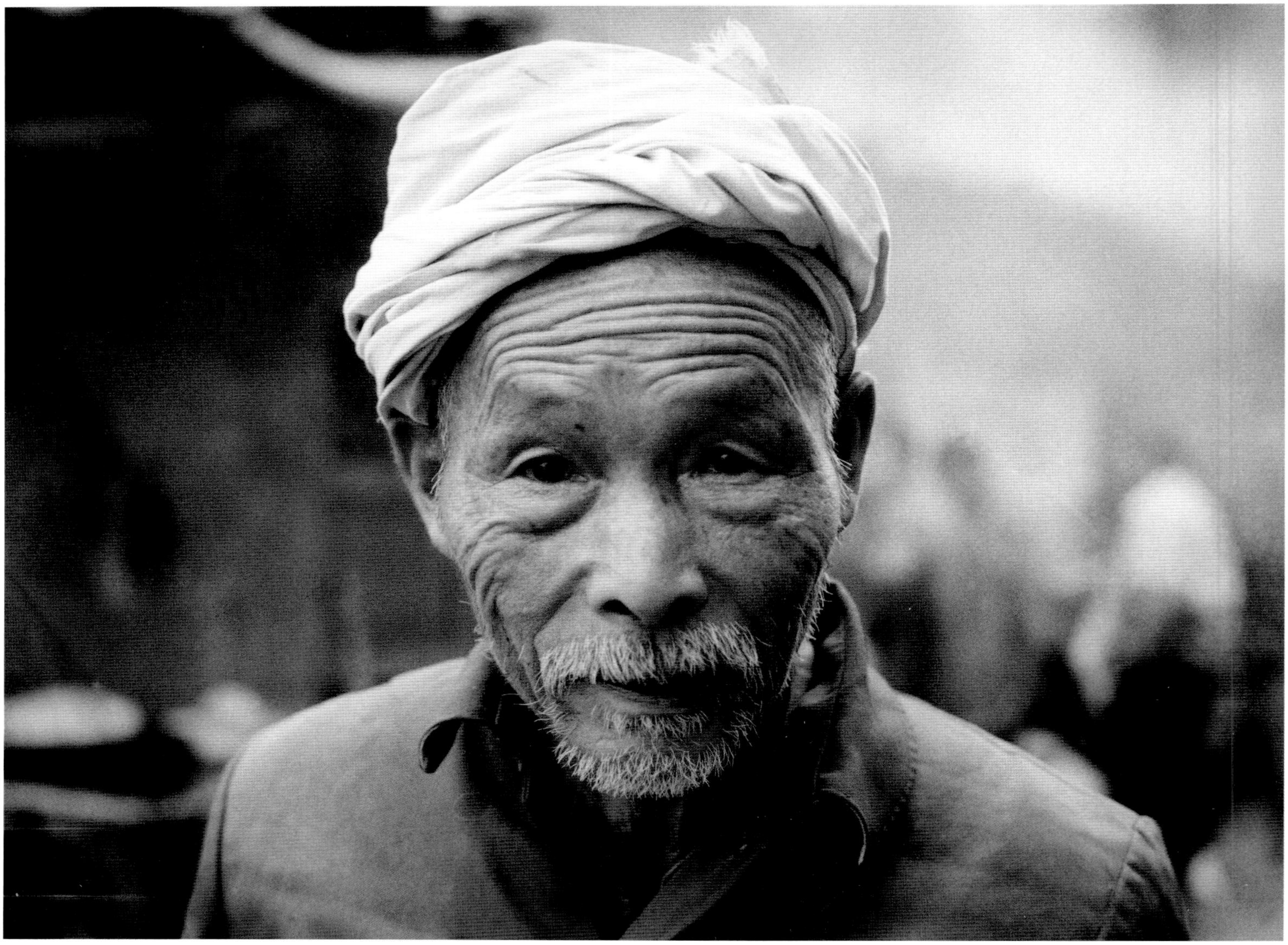

Chungqing 1992

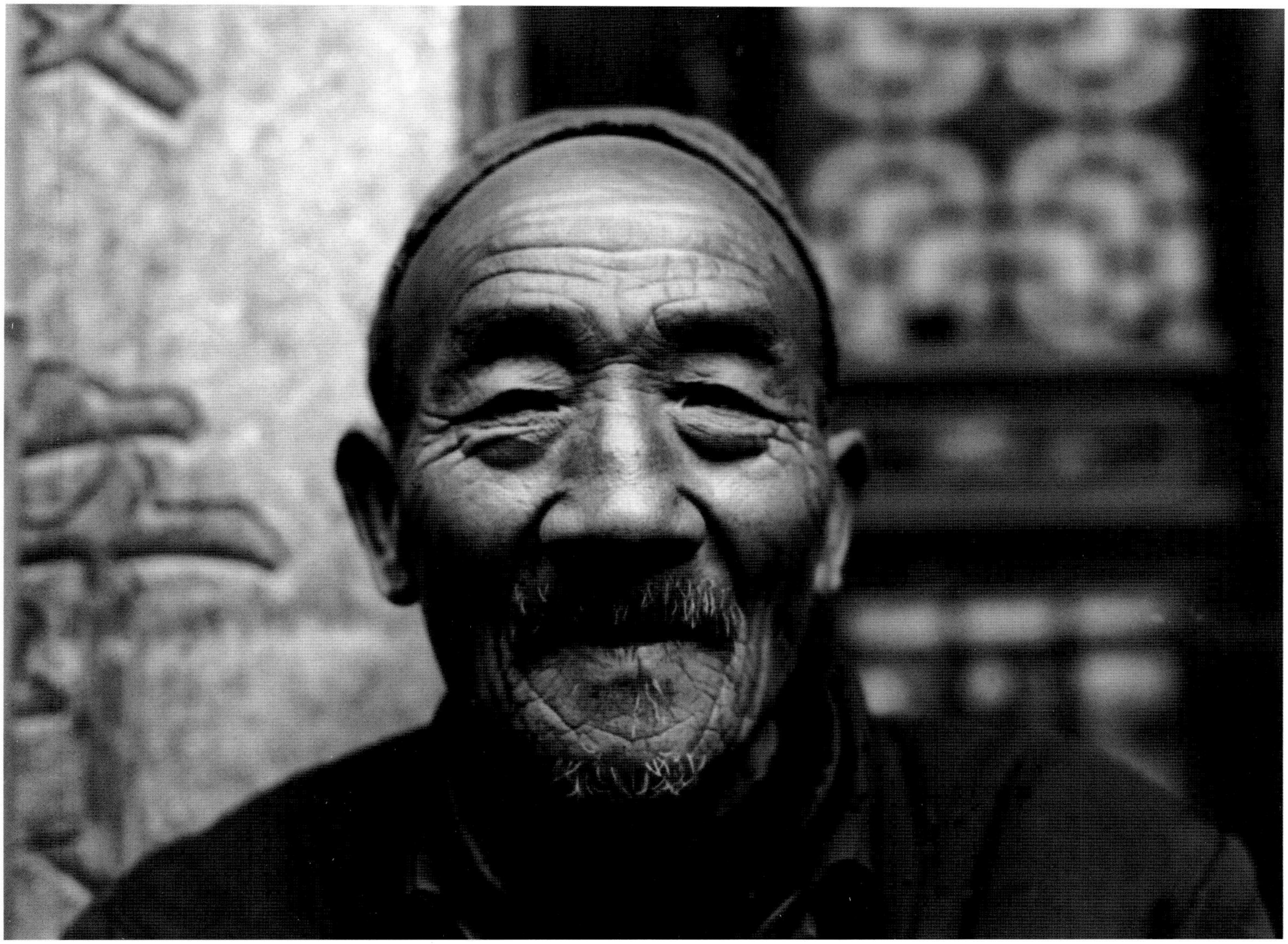

Shanxi 1995

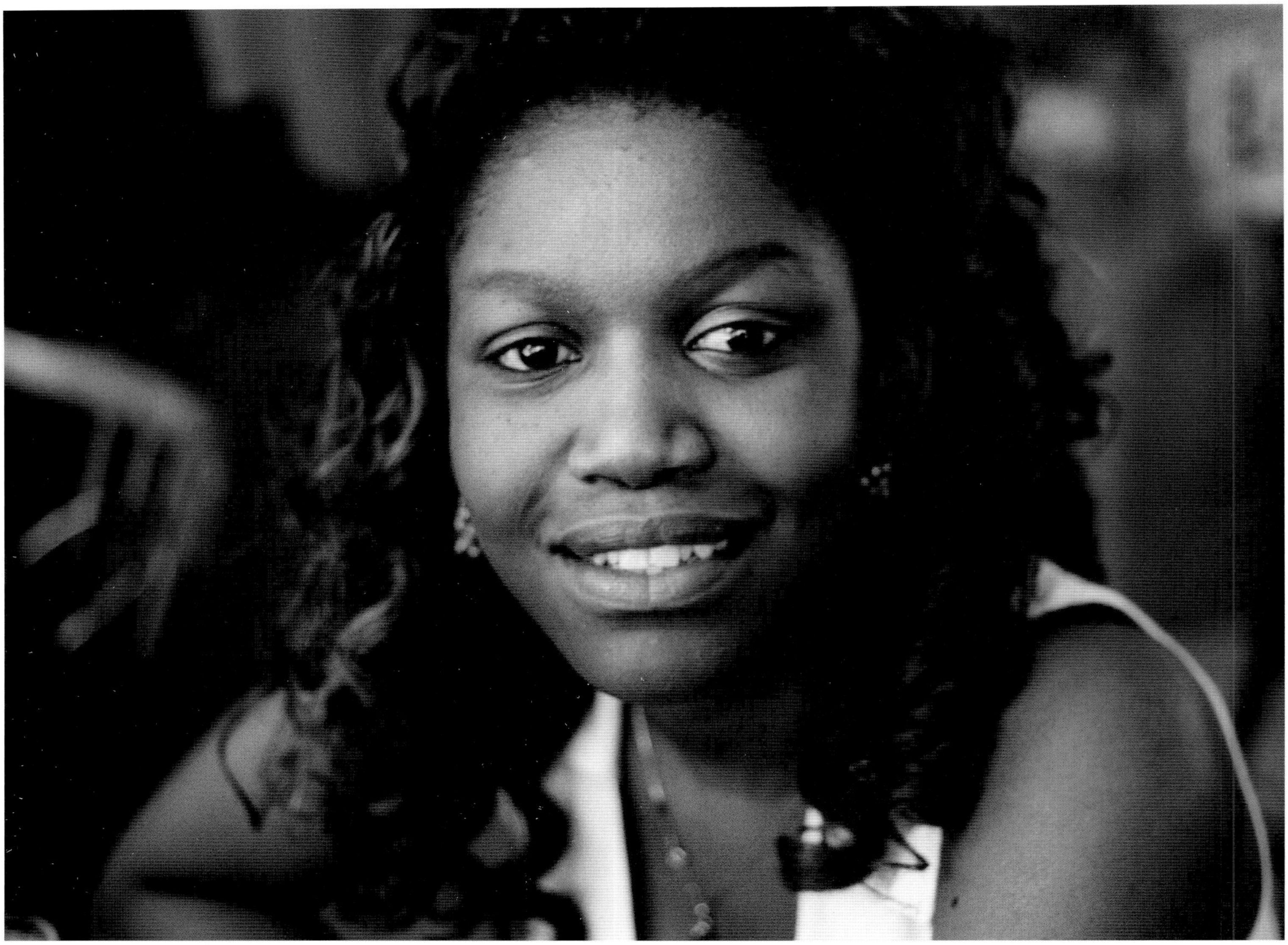

New Orleans 1999

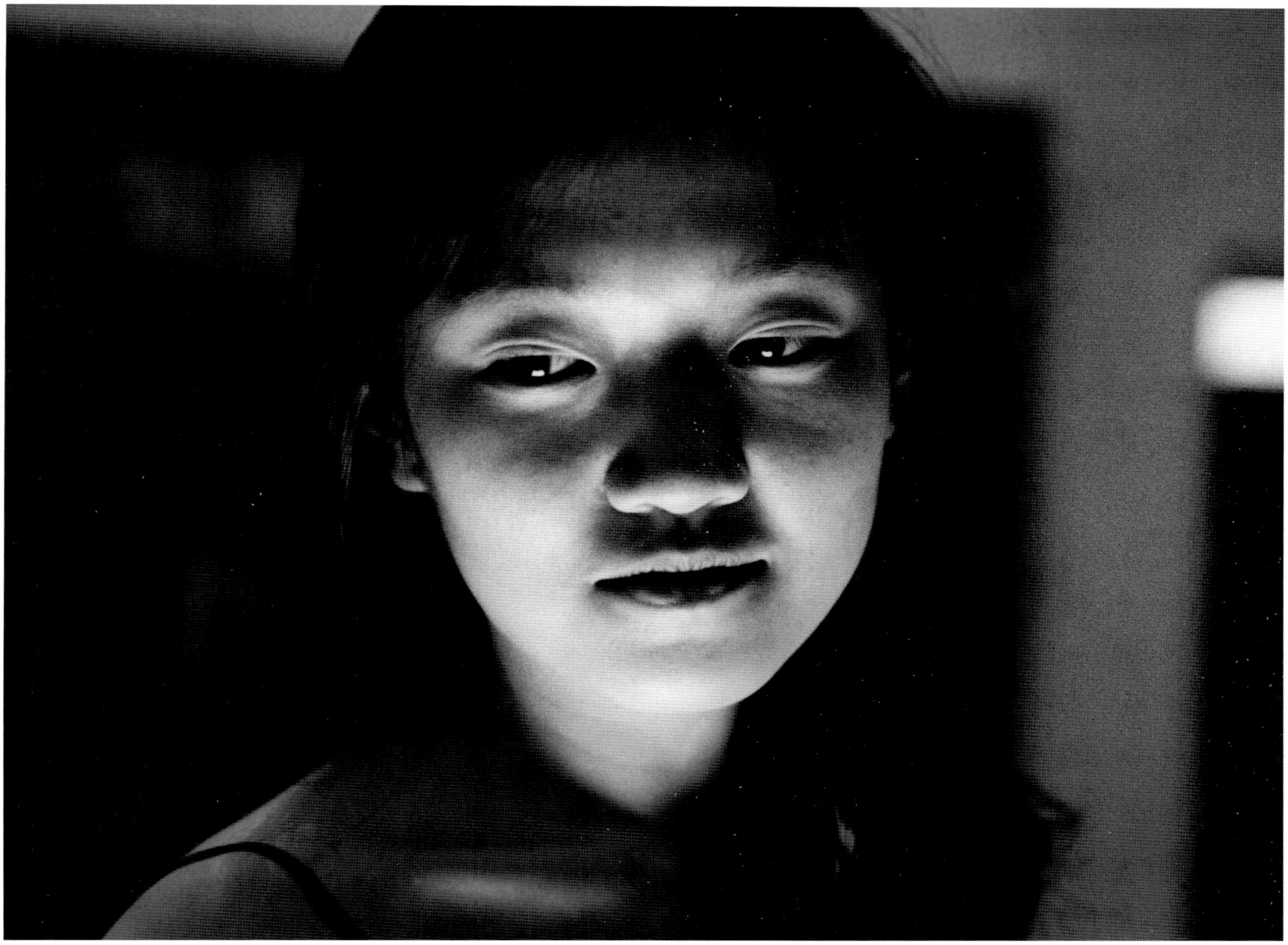

Beijing 1998

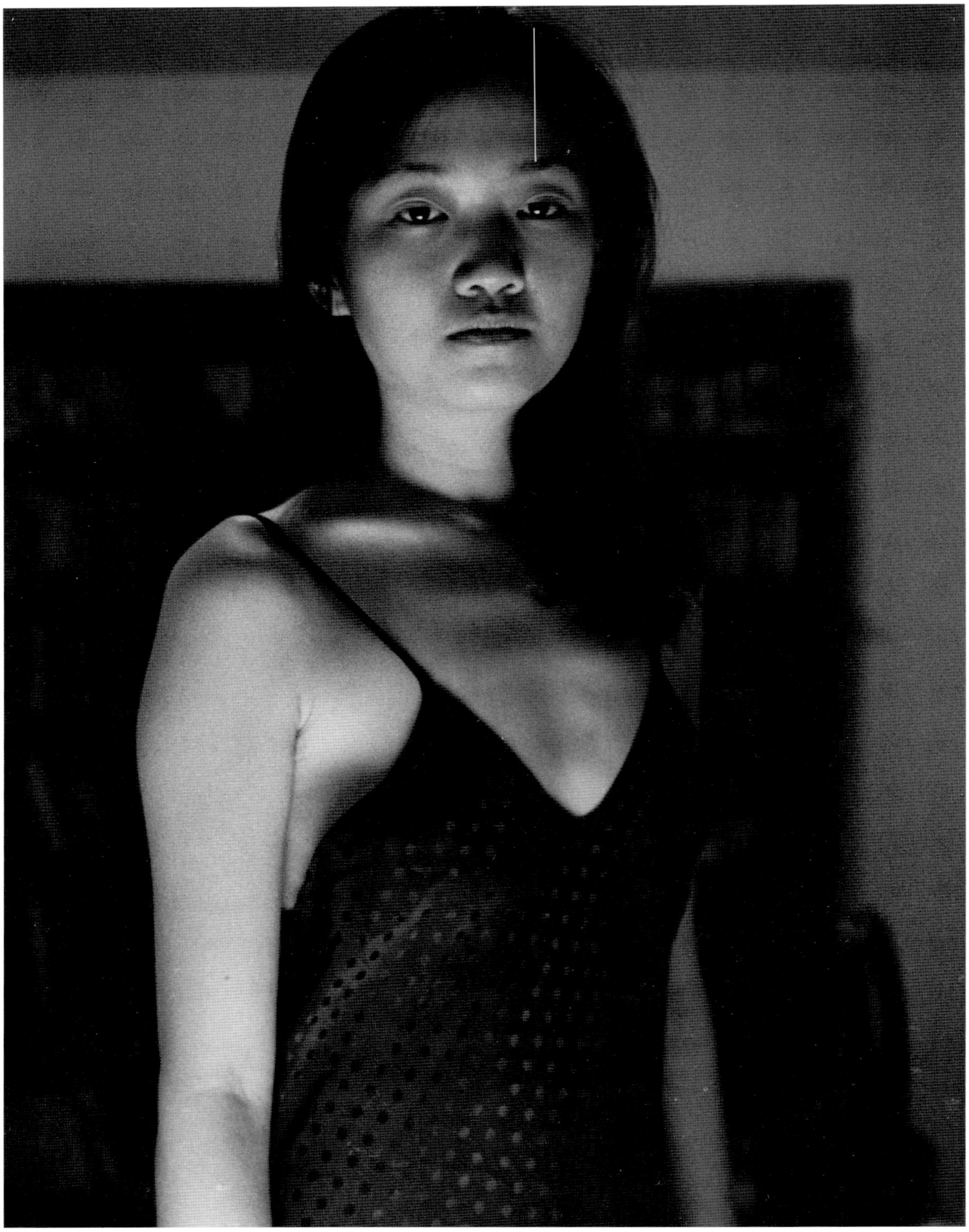

Beijing 1998

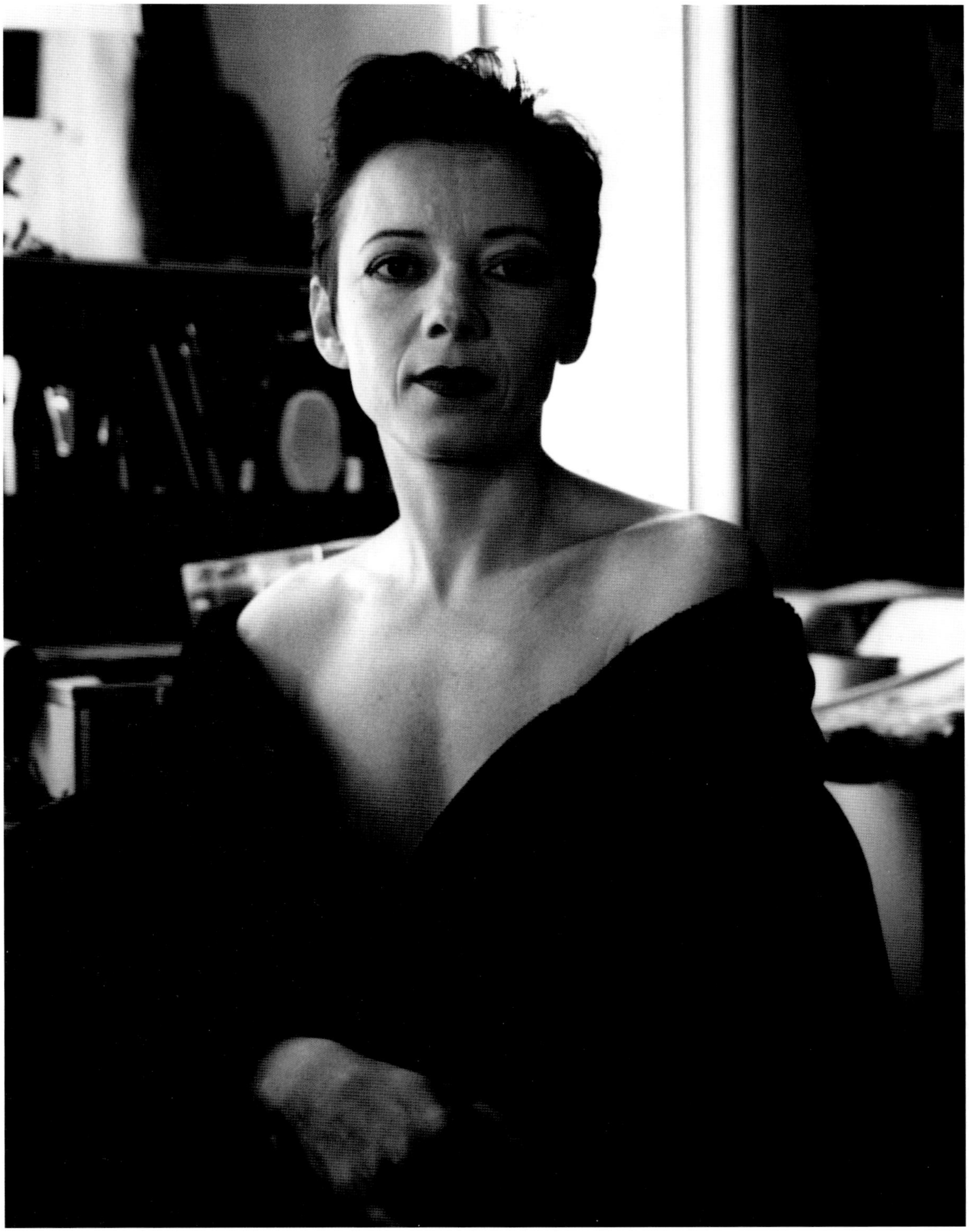

Munich 1994

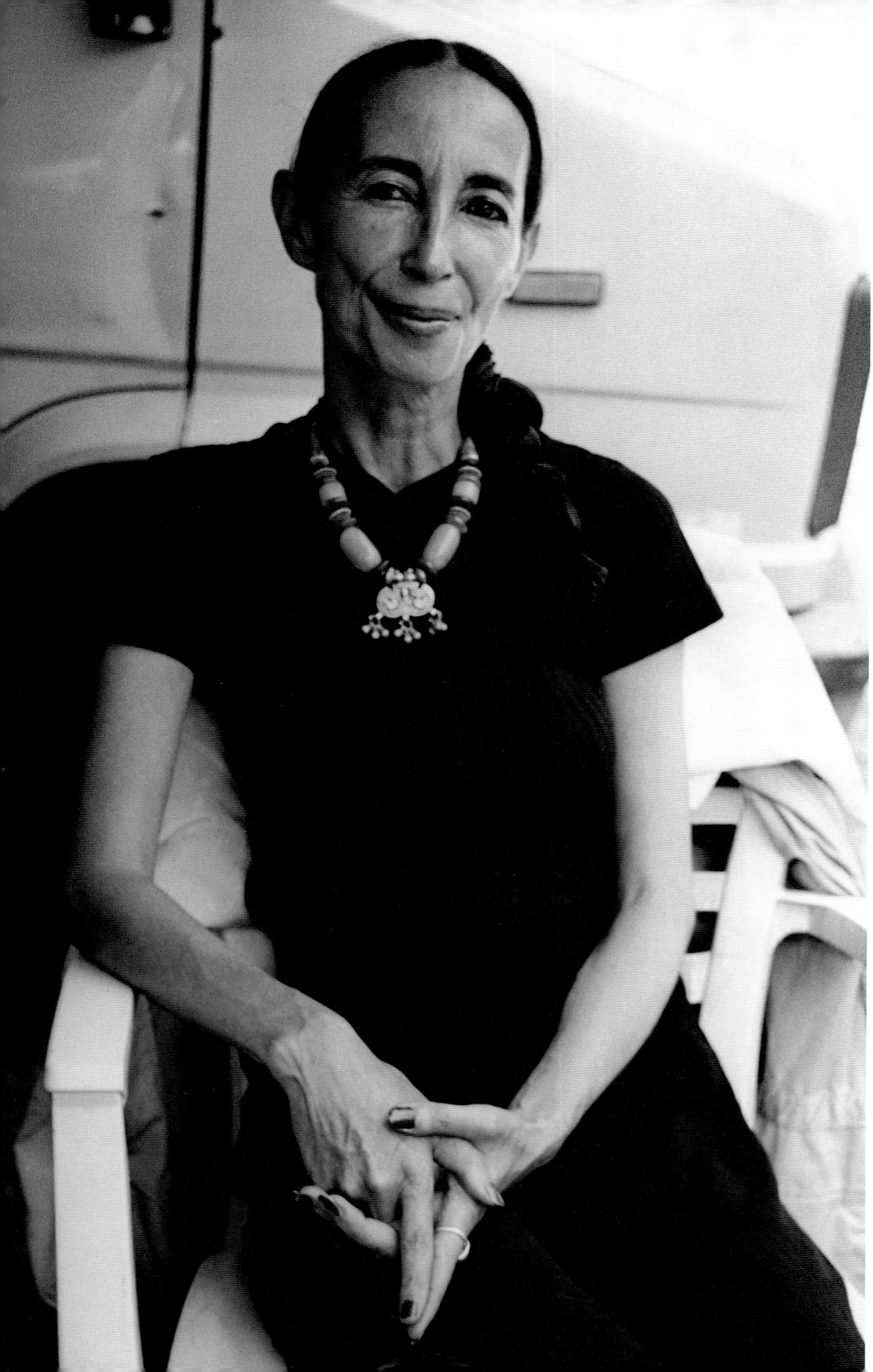

Lisbon 1999

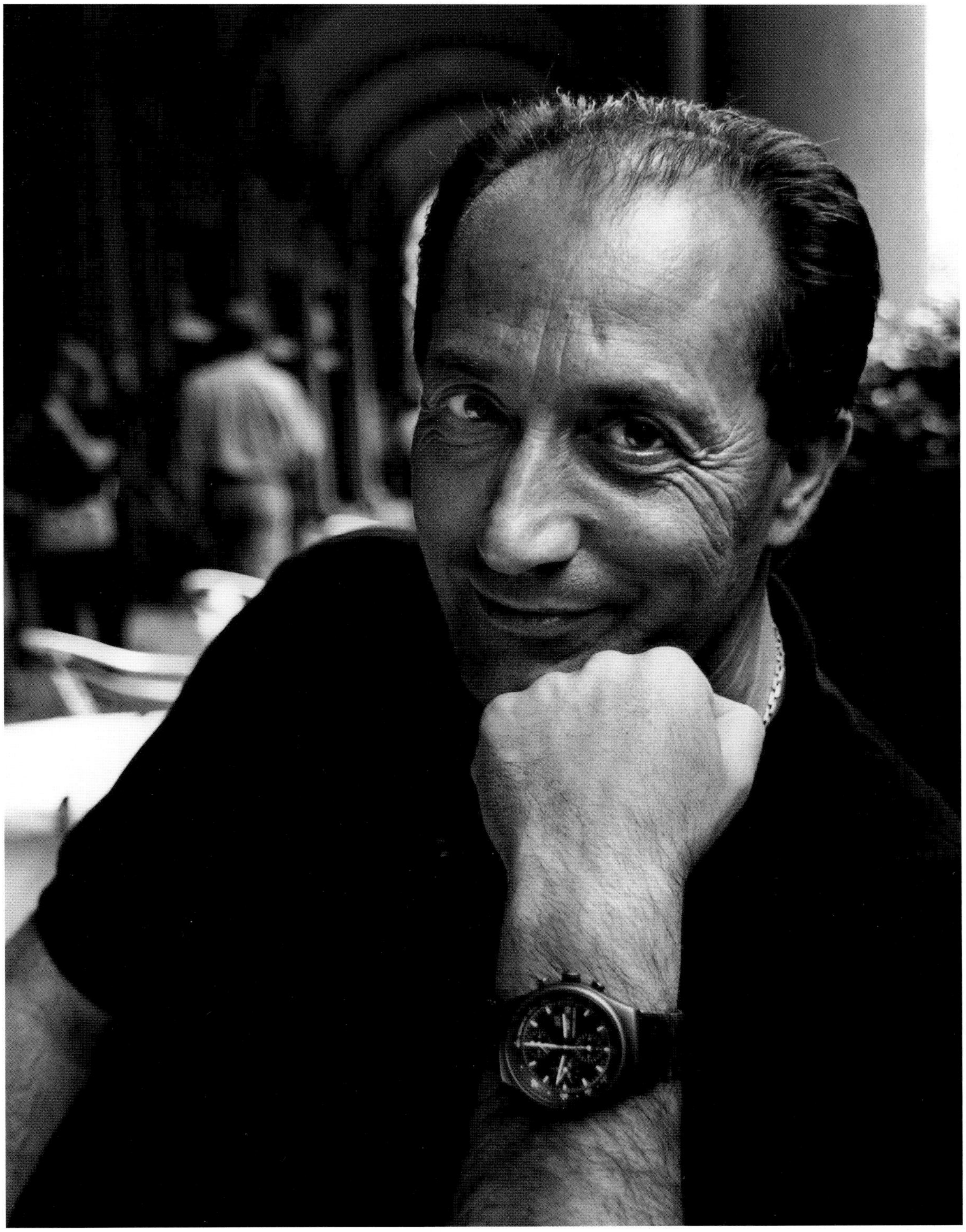

Bologna 1999

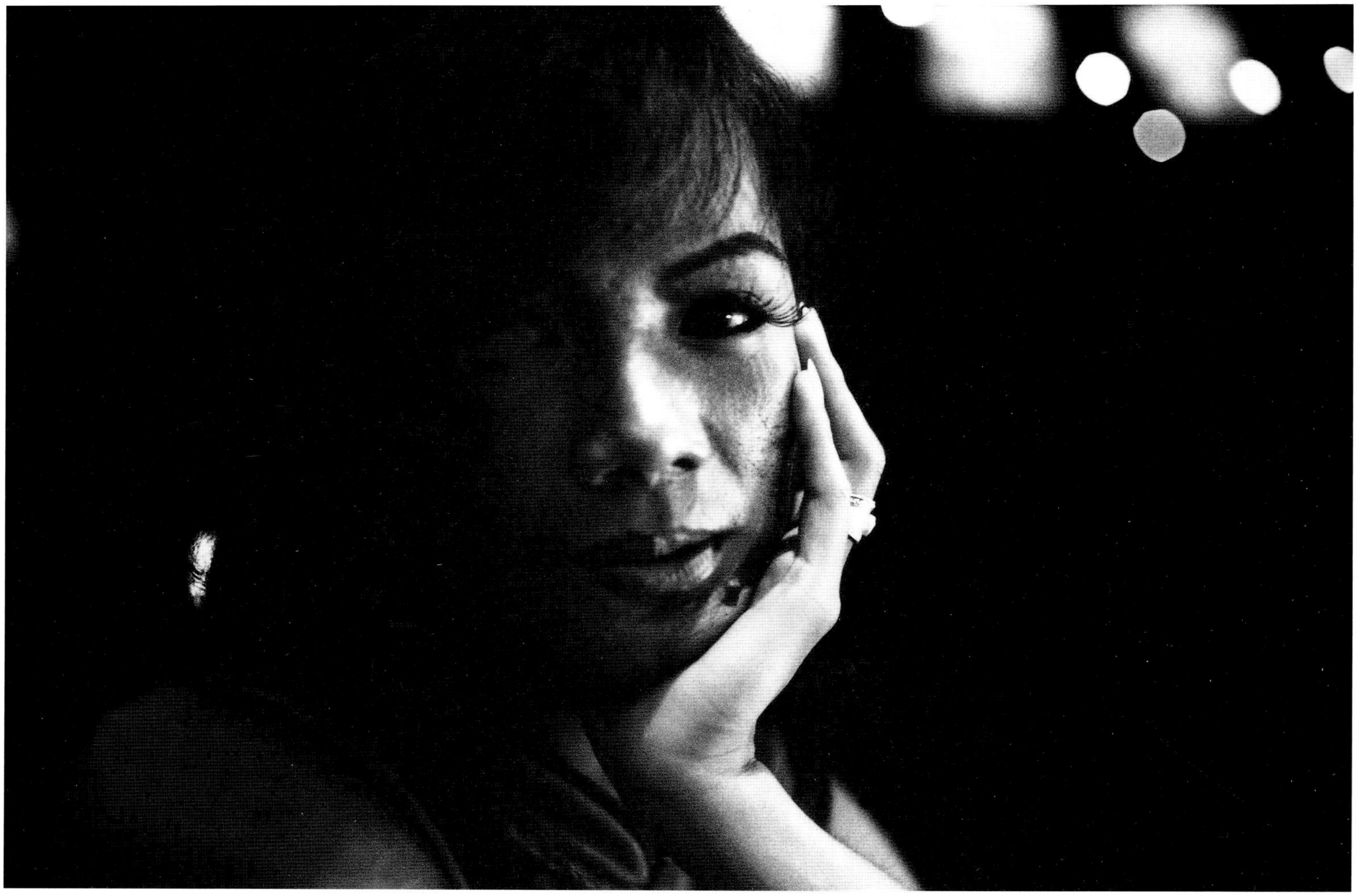

Koh Samai 1993

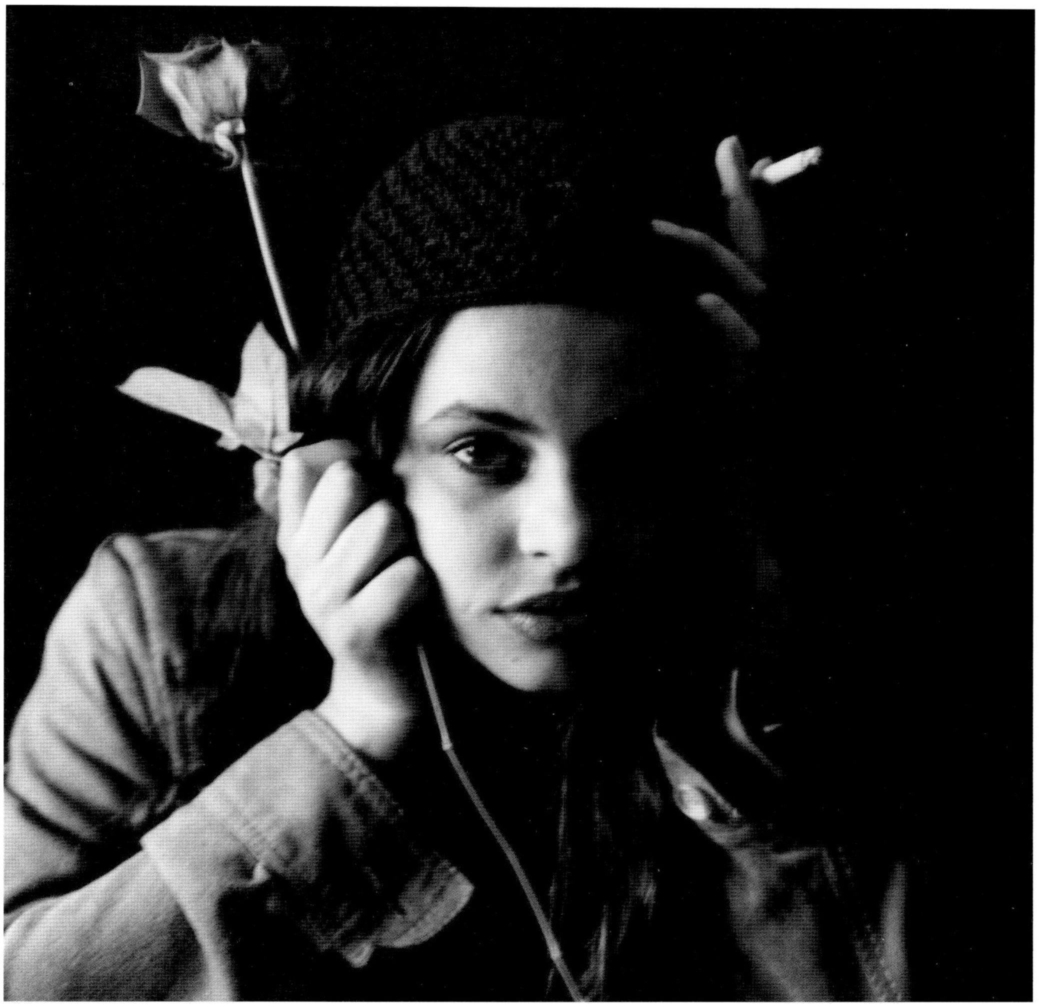

New York 1994

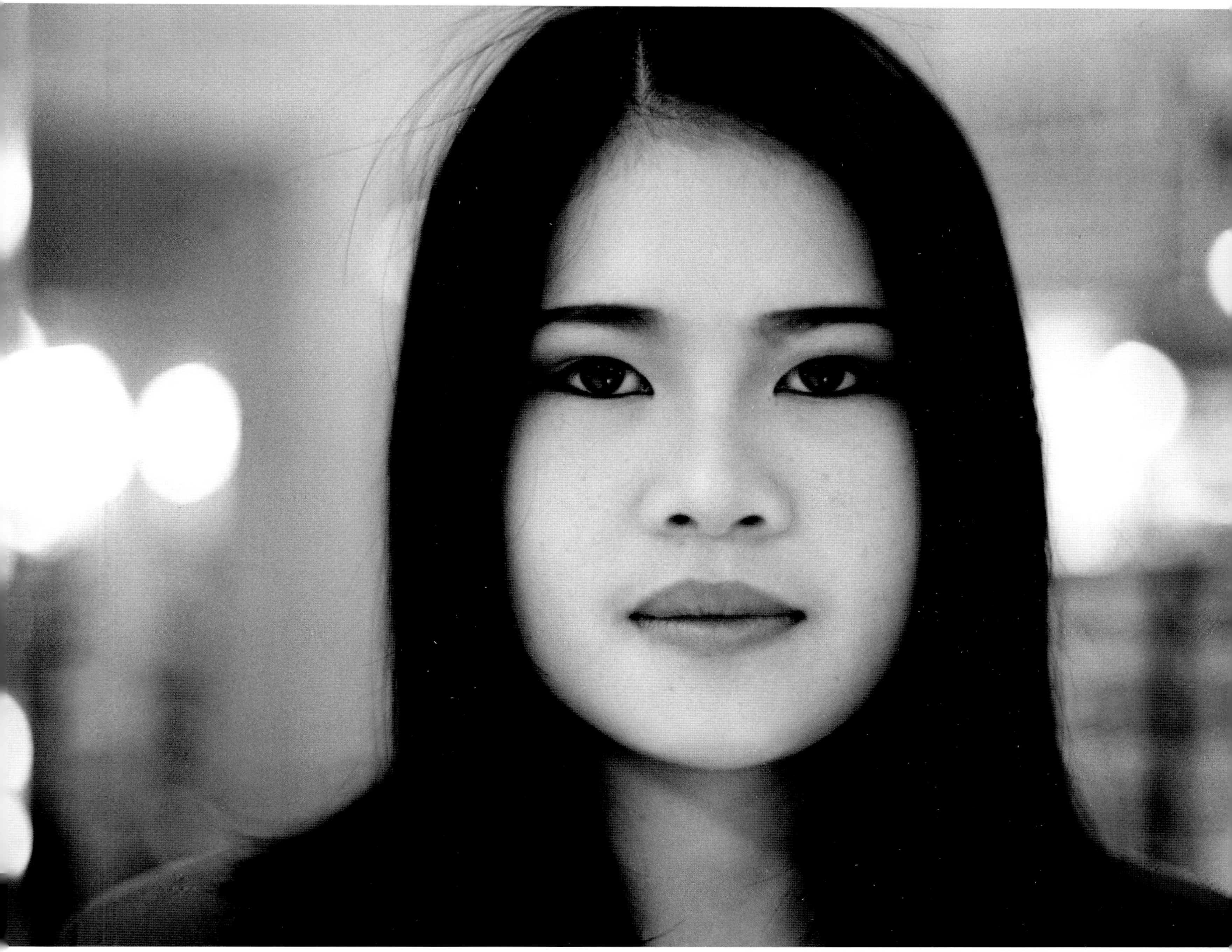

Bangkok 1993

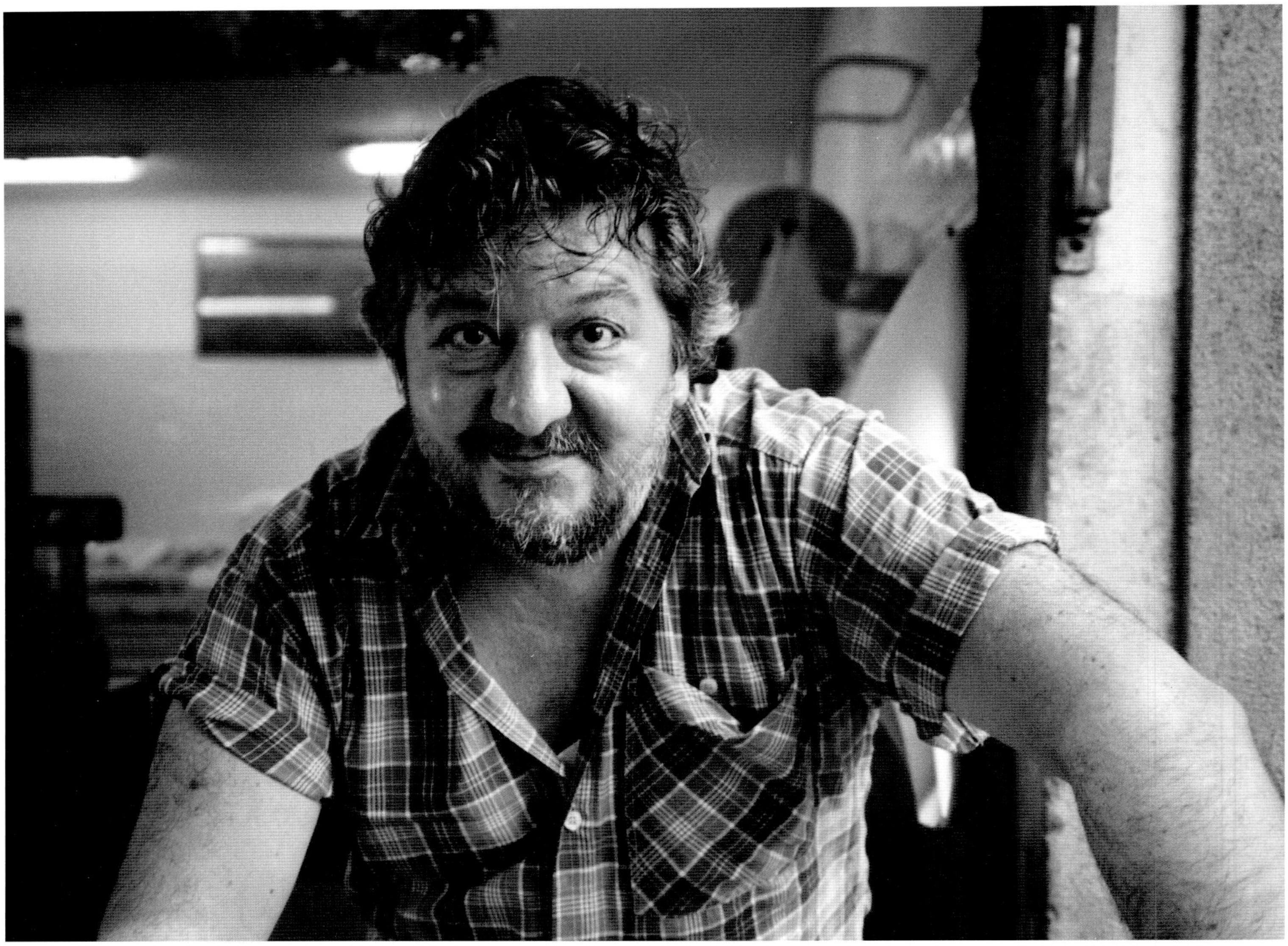

Naples 1998

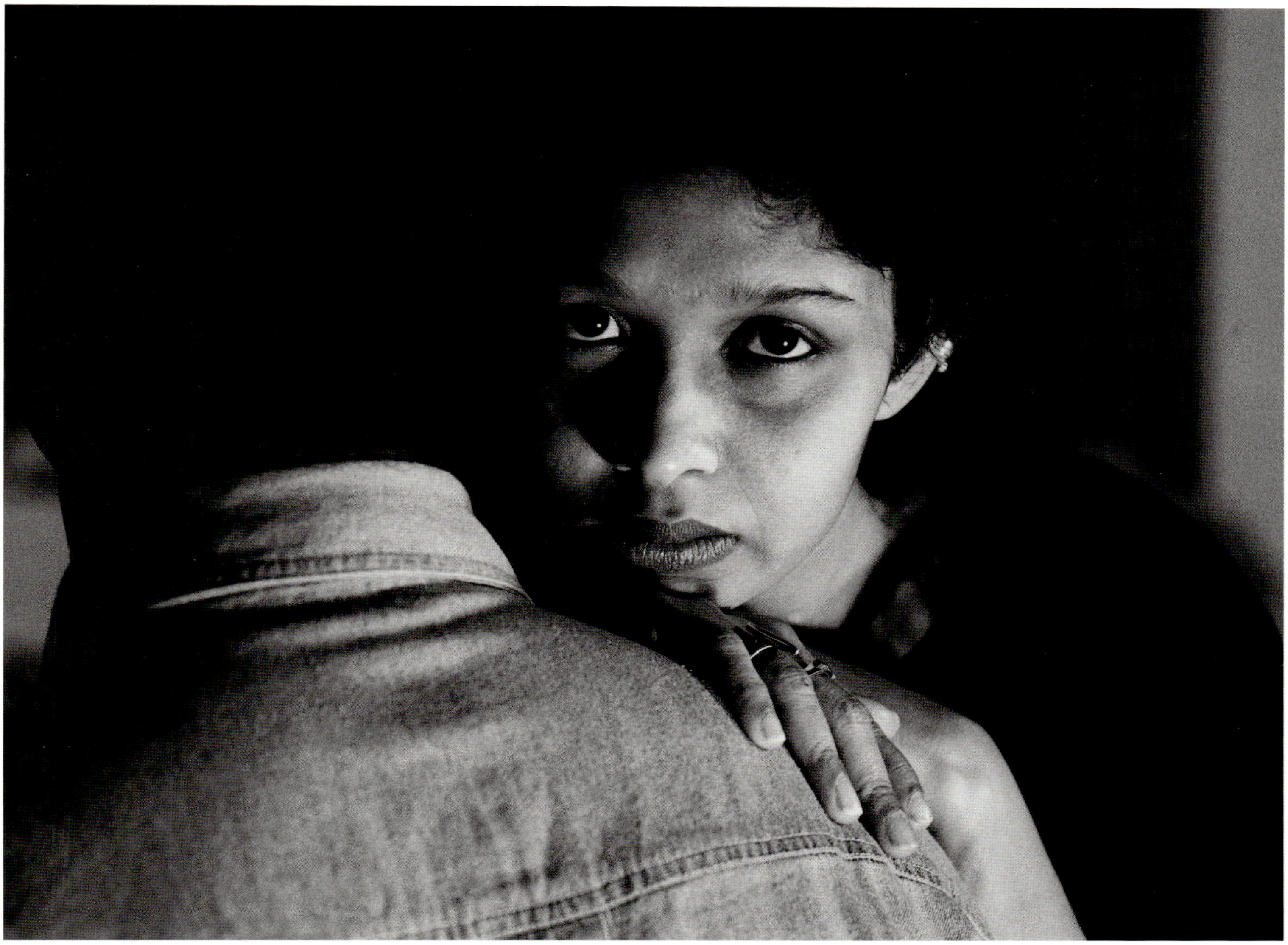

Munich 1992

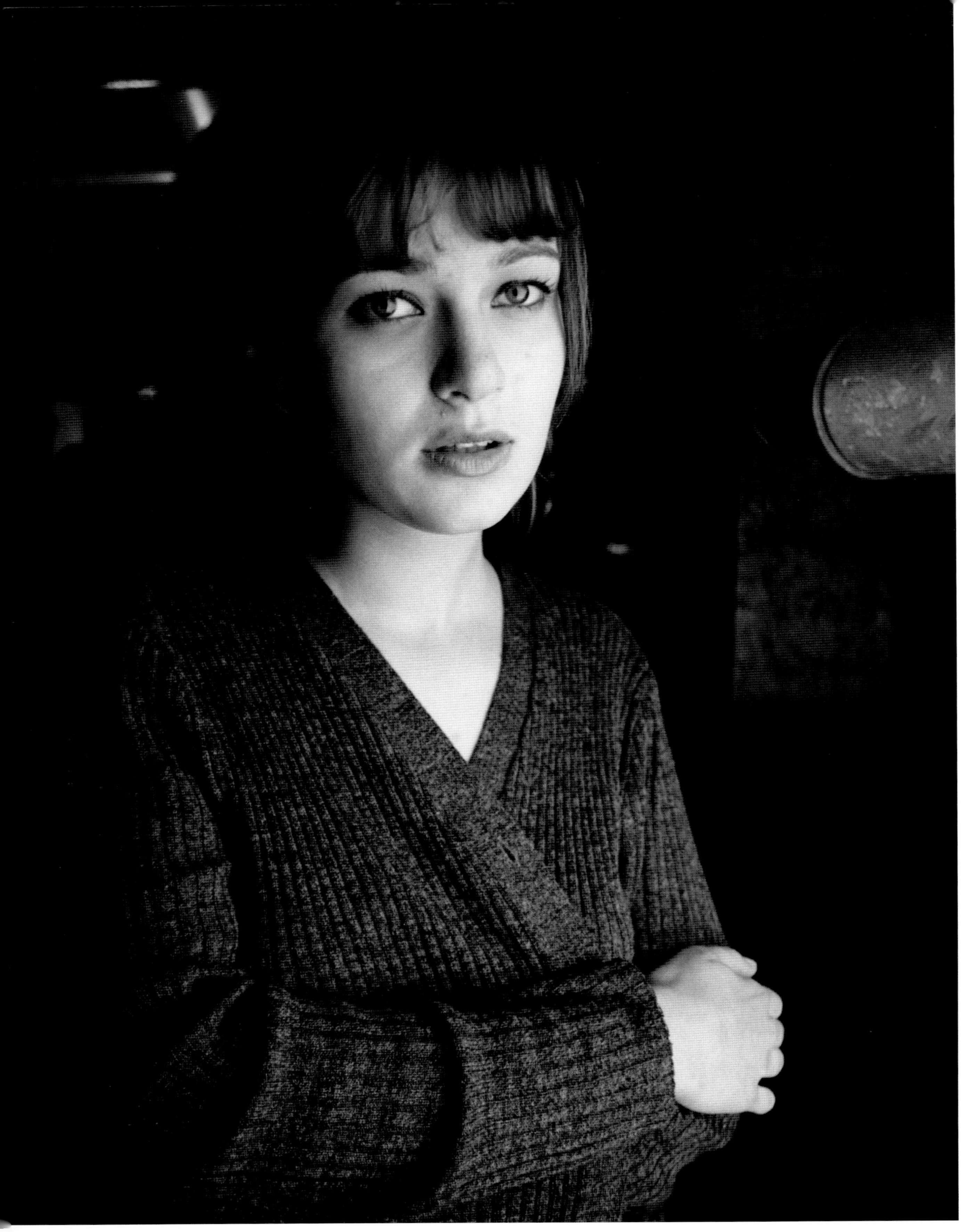

Herten 1998

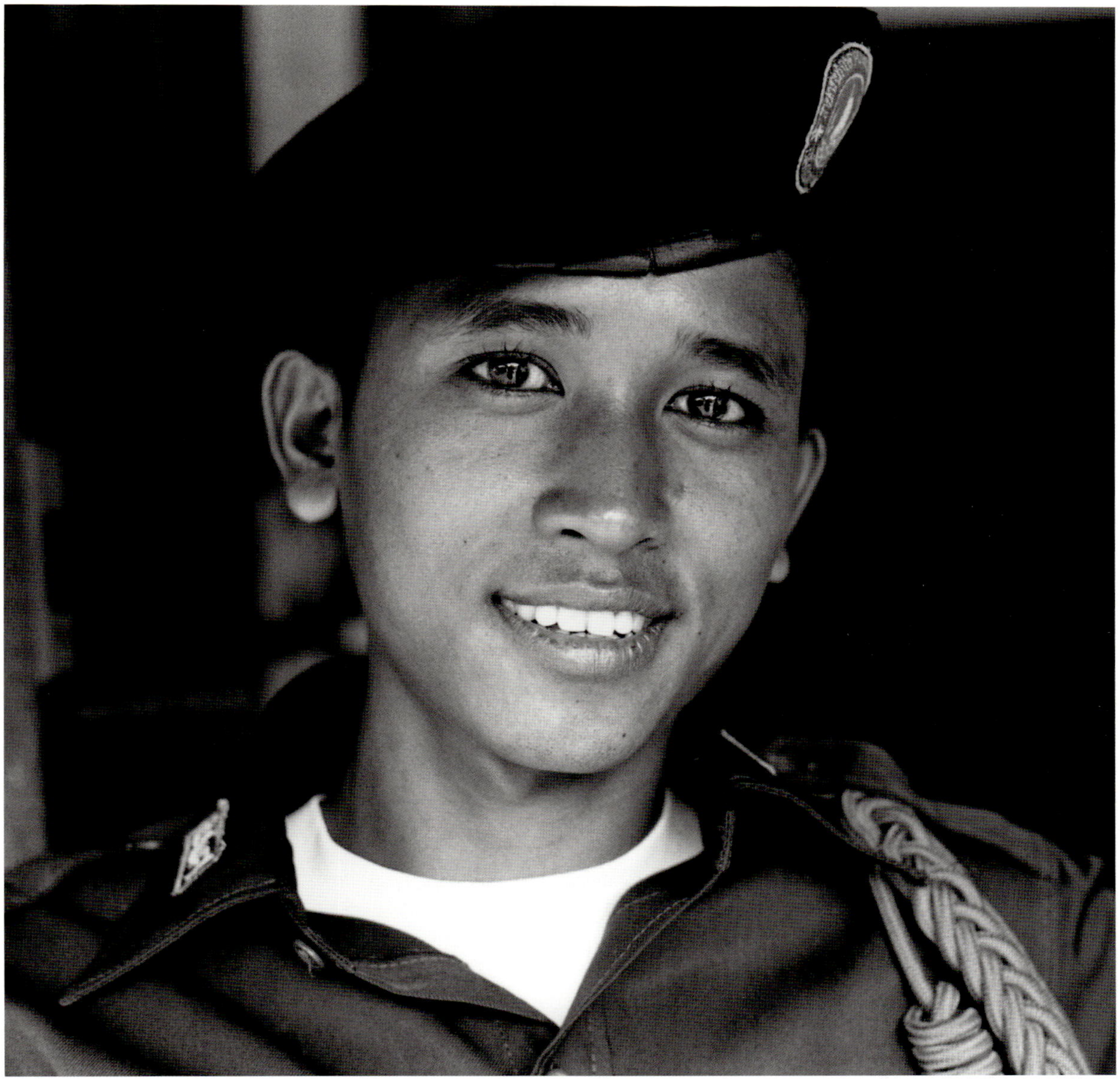

Bangkok 1993

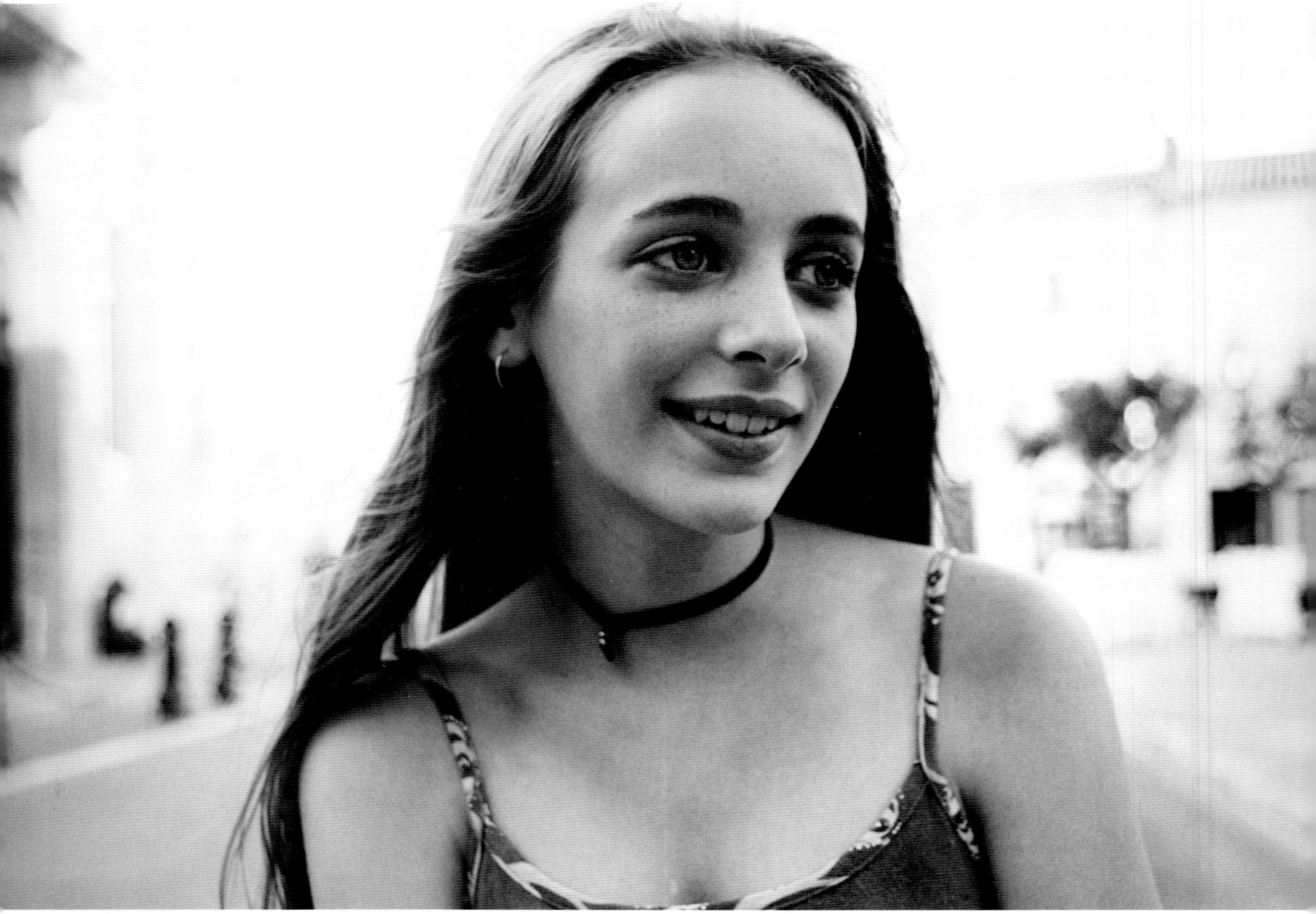

Aix-en-Provence 1999

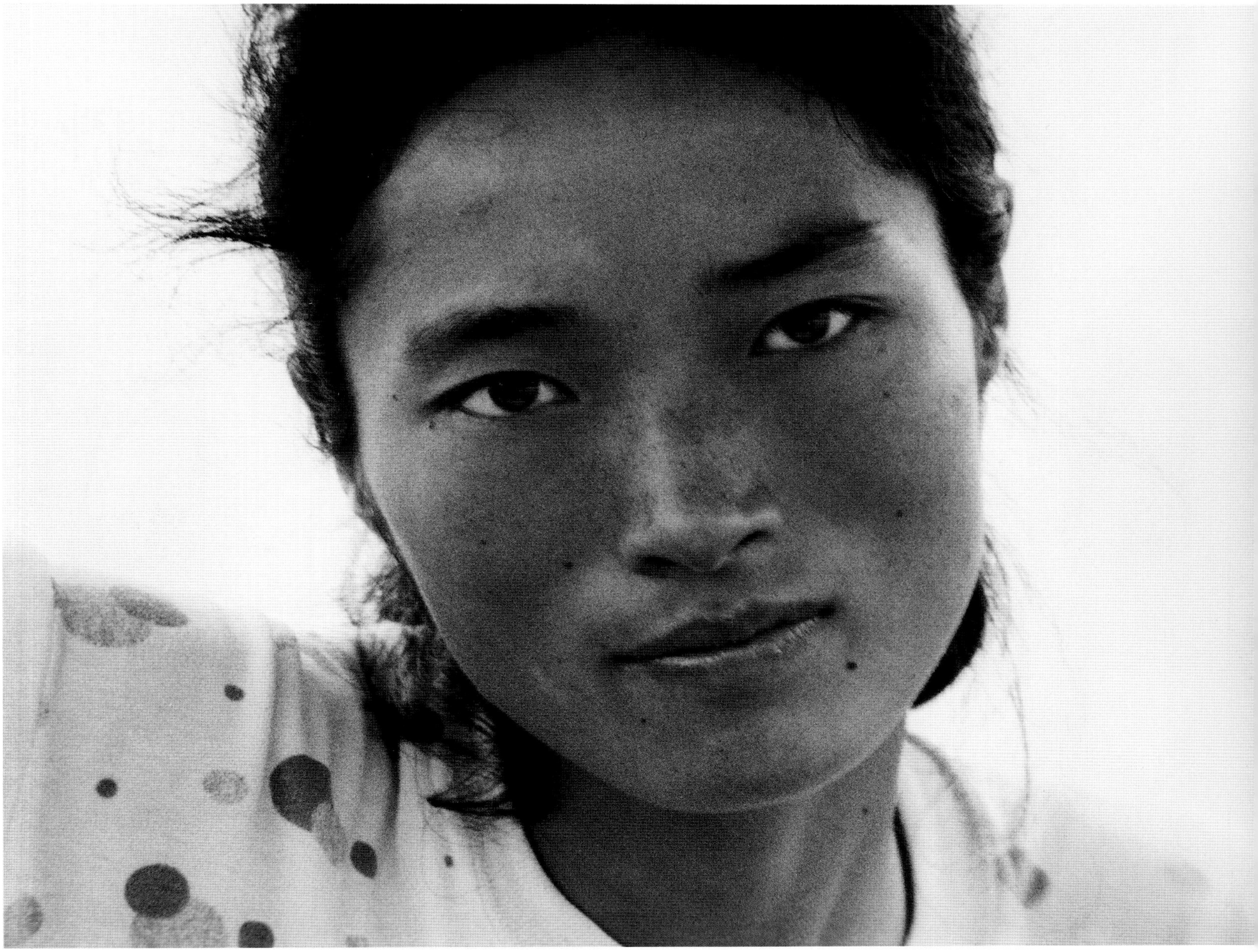

Wuhan 1992

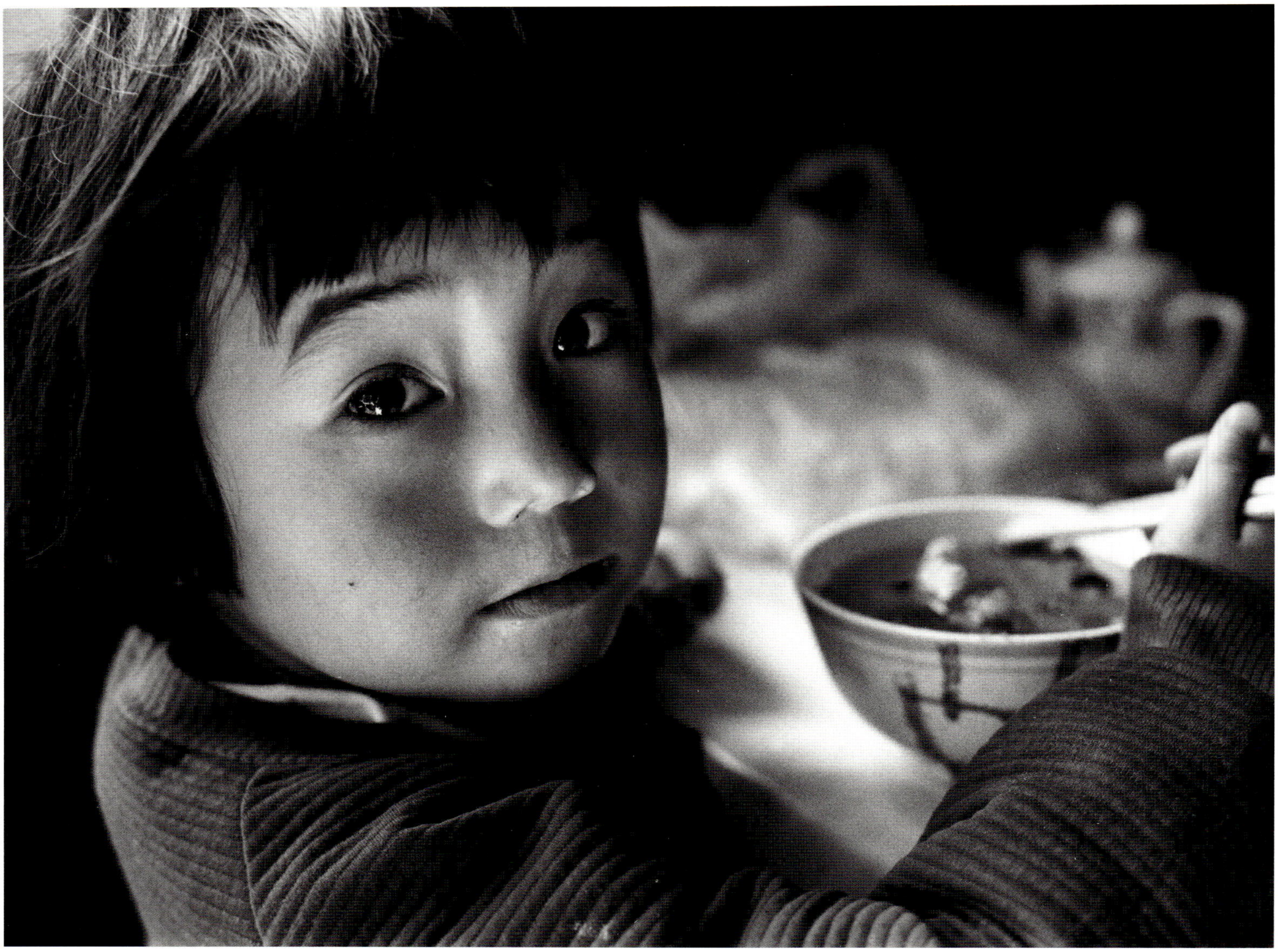

Beijing 1992

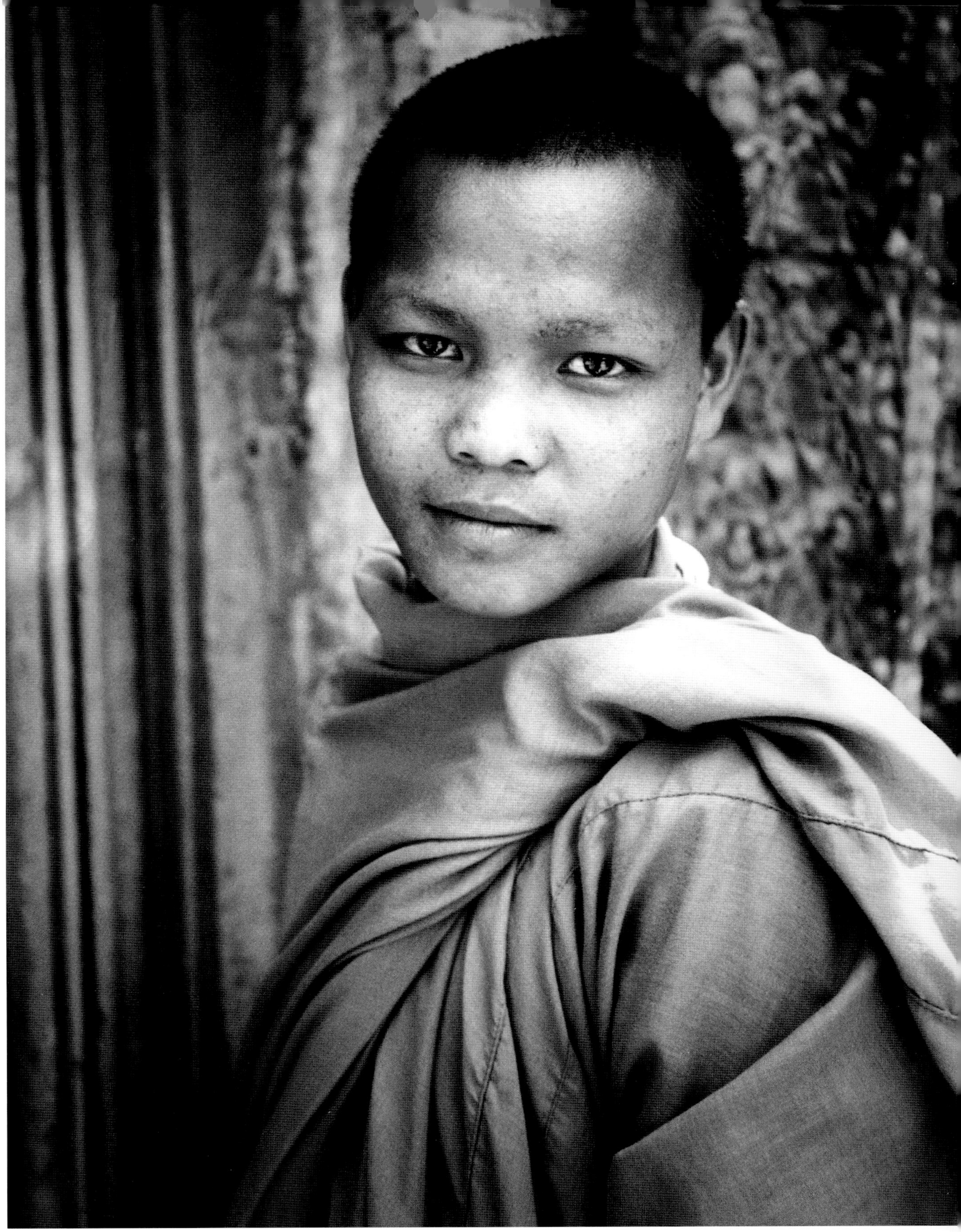

Angkor 2000

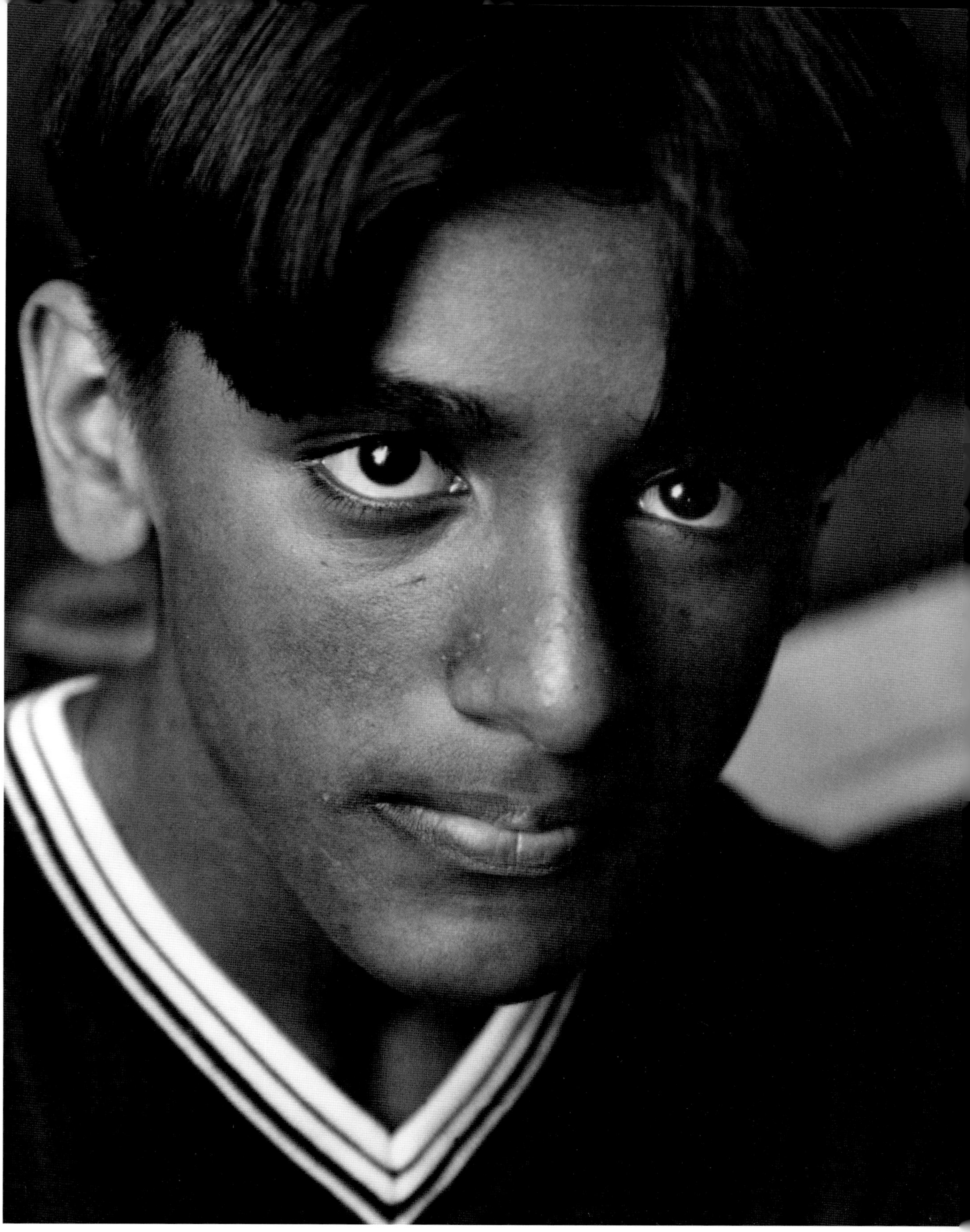

London 1997

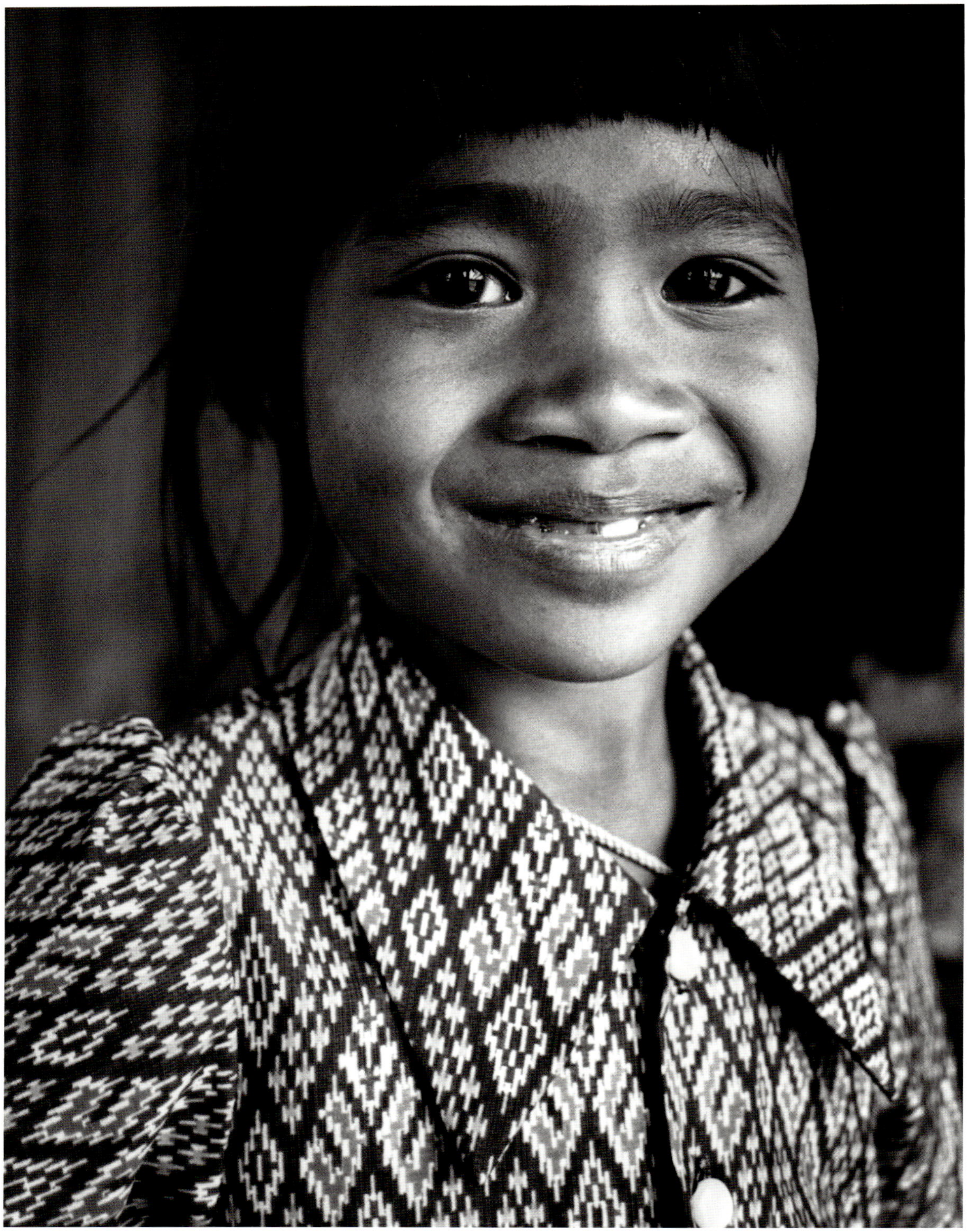

Sisophon 2000

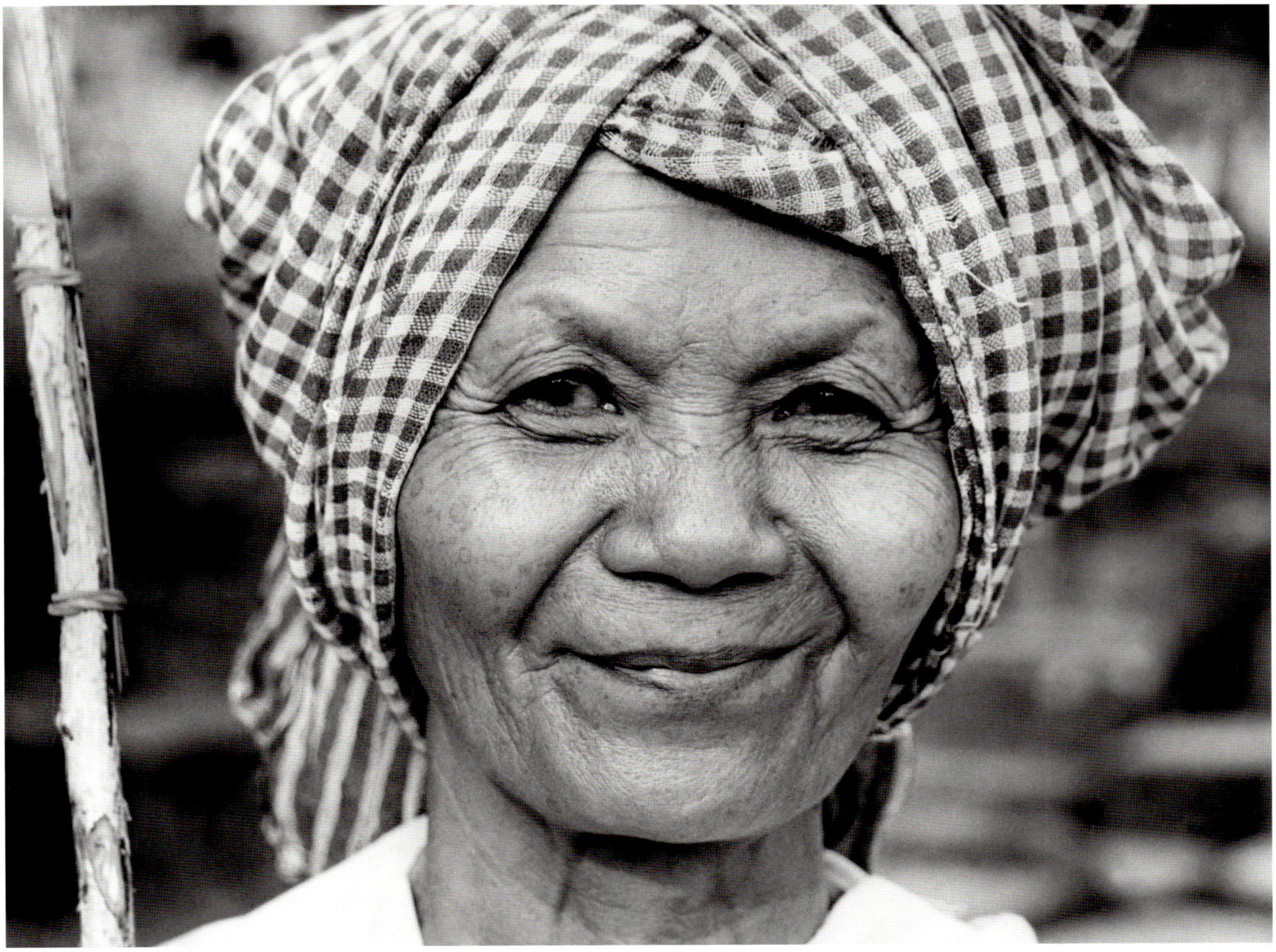

Poipet 2000

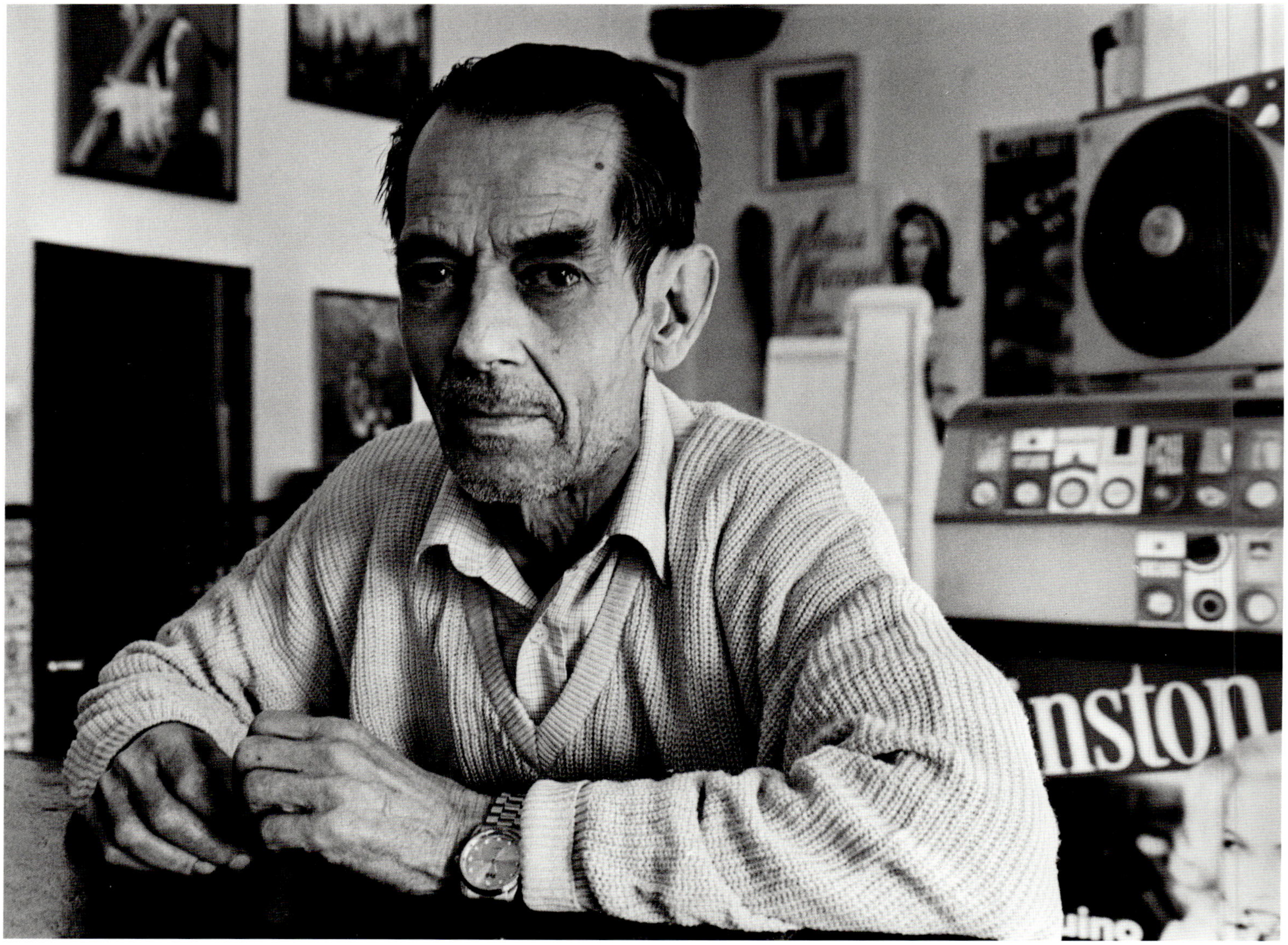

Tarifa 1998

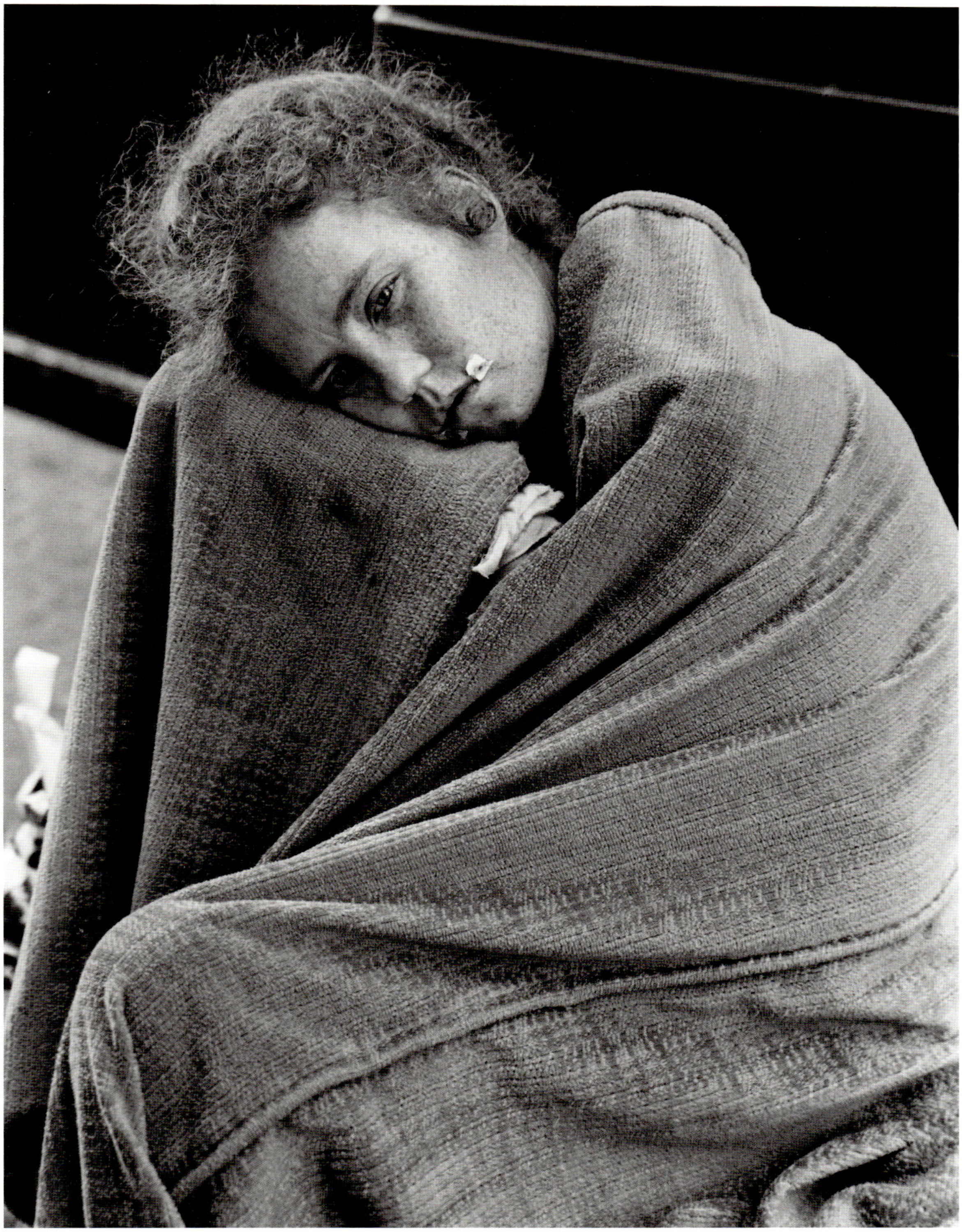

Seville 1998

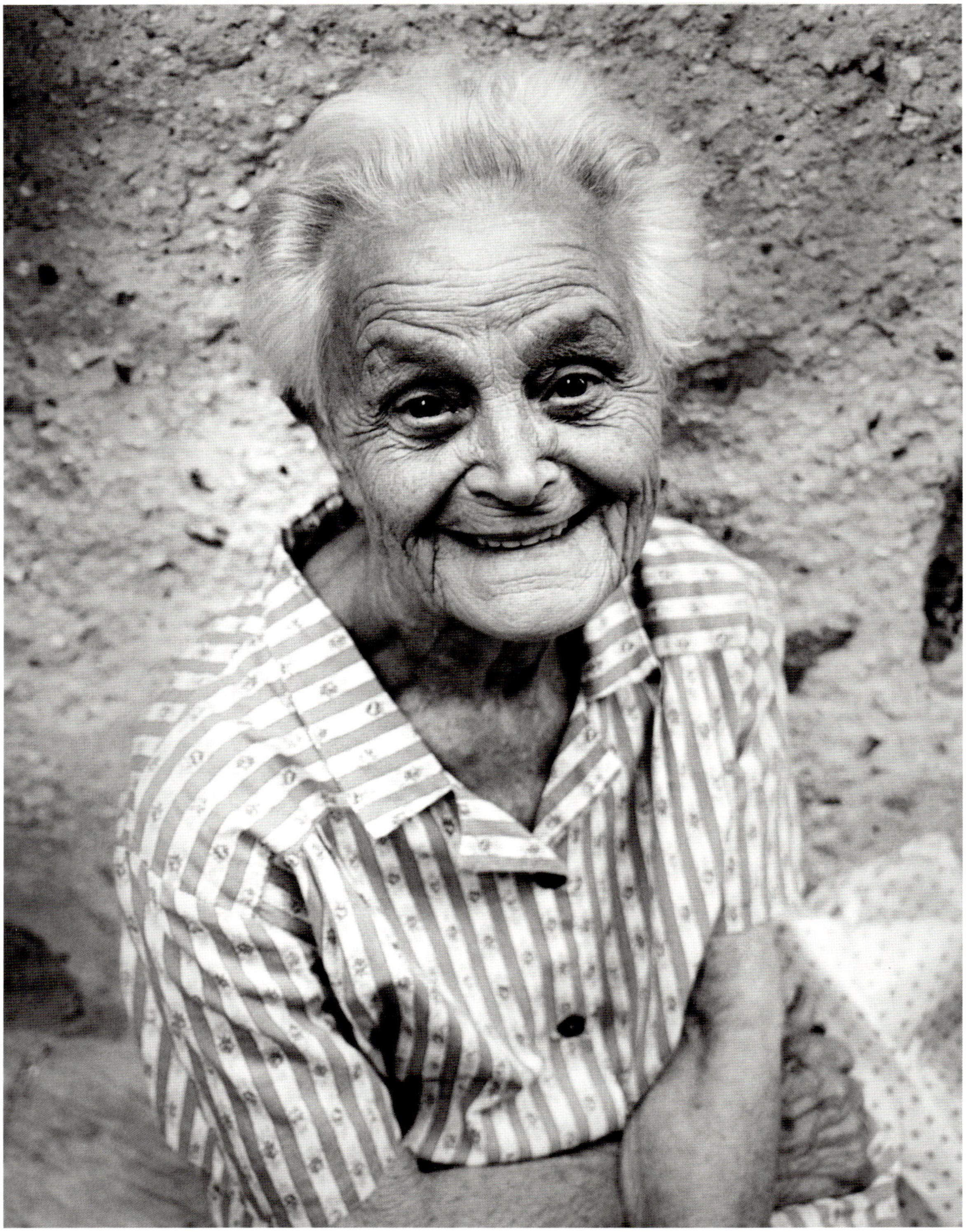

Naples 1999

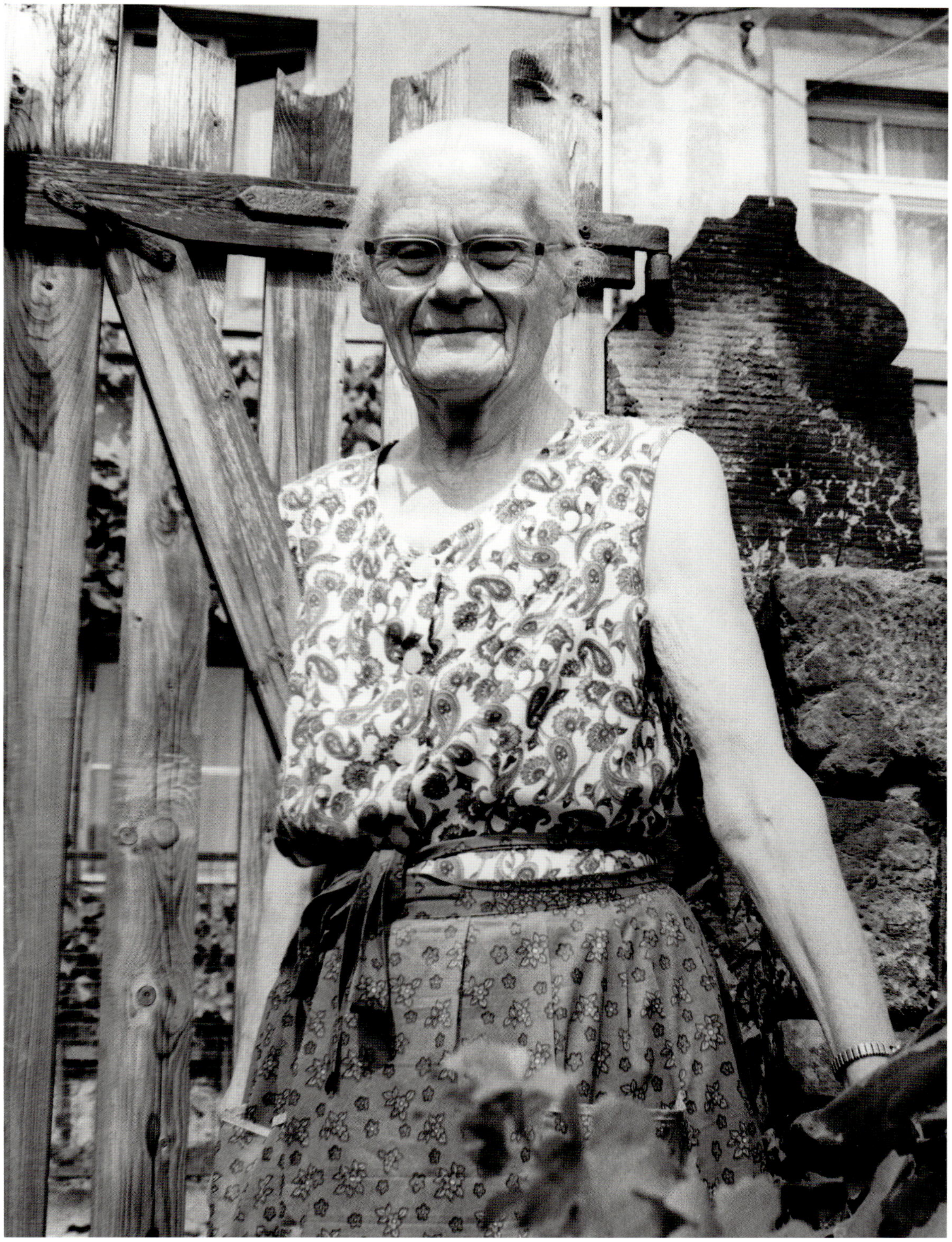

Saxony 1991

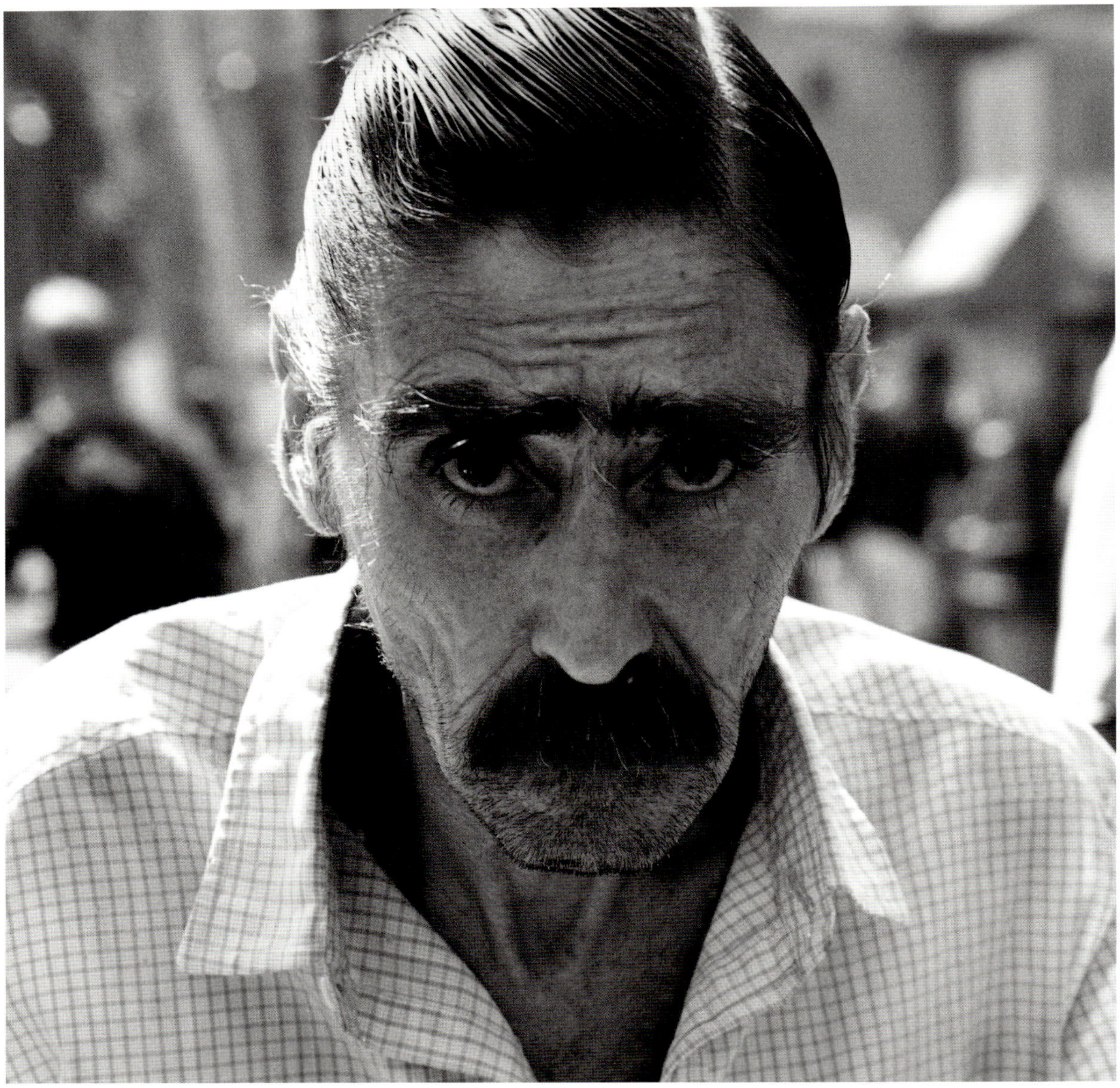

Barcelona 1998

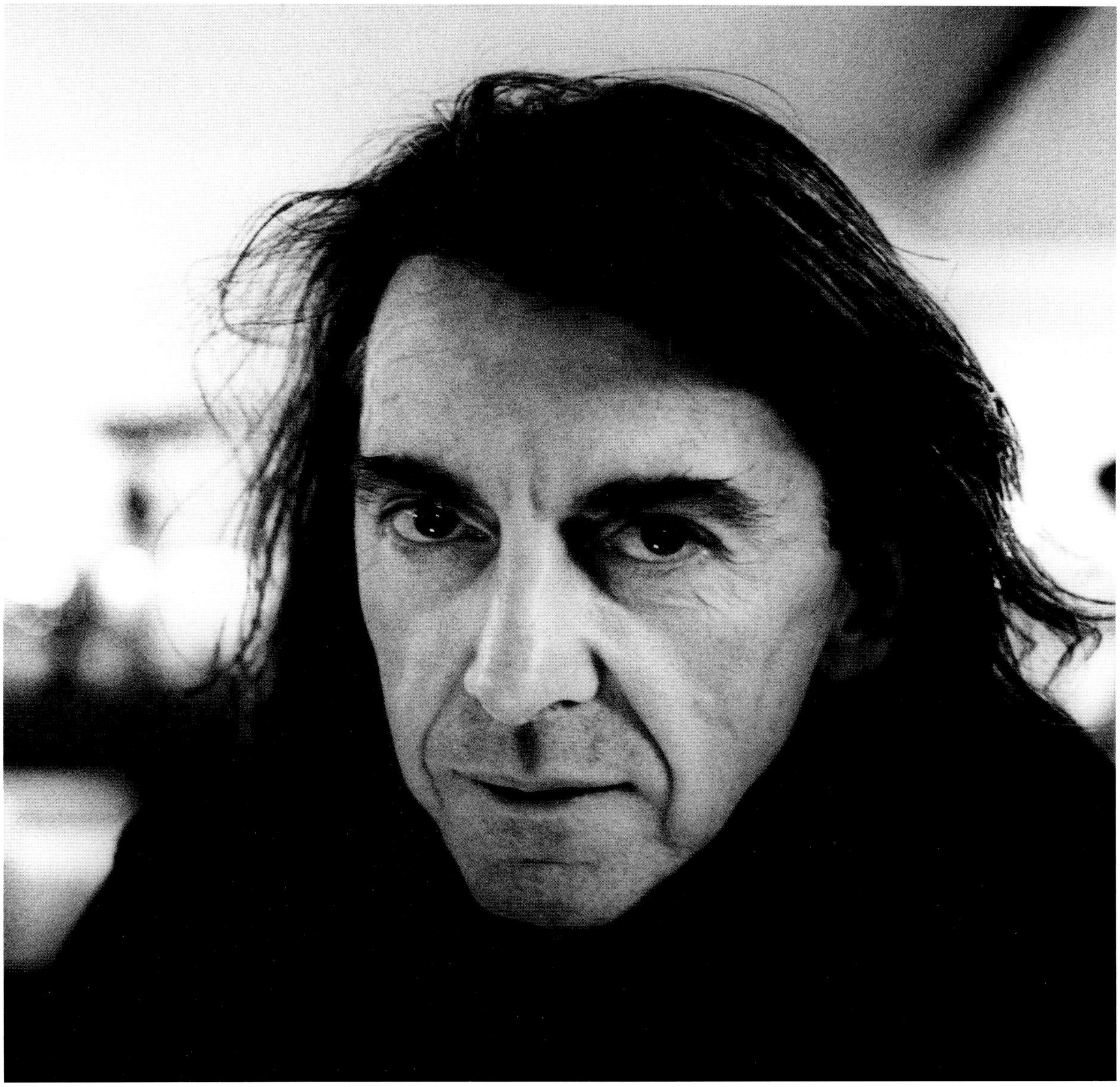

Munich 1999

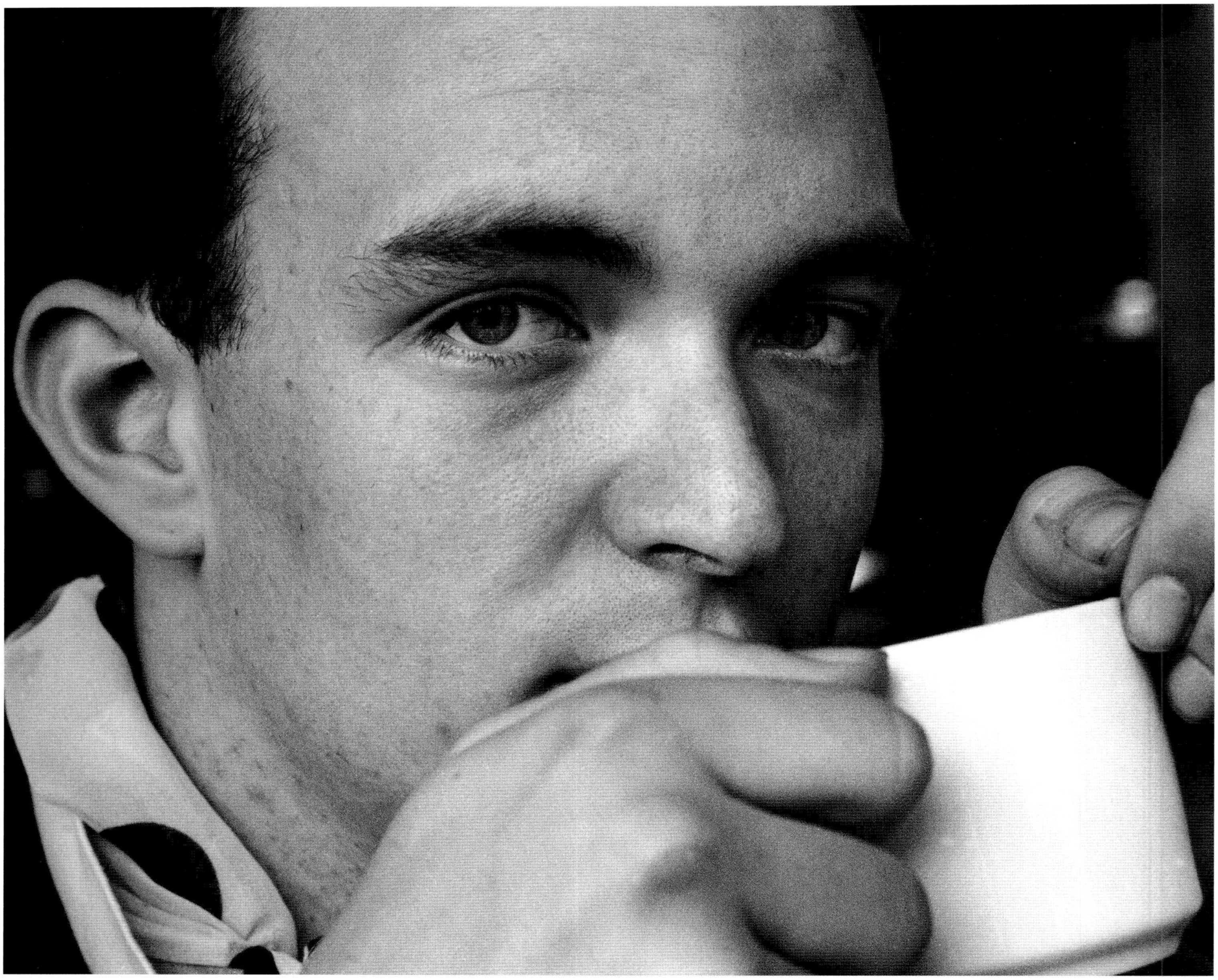

Prague 1993

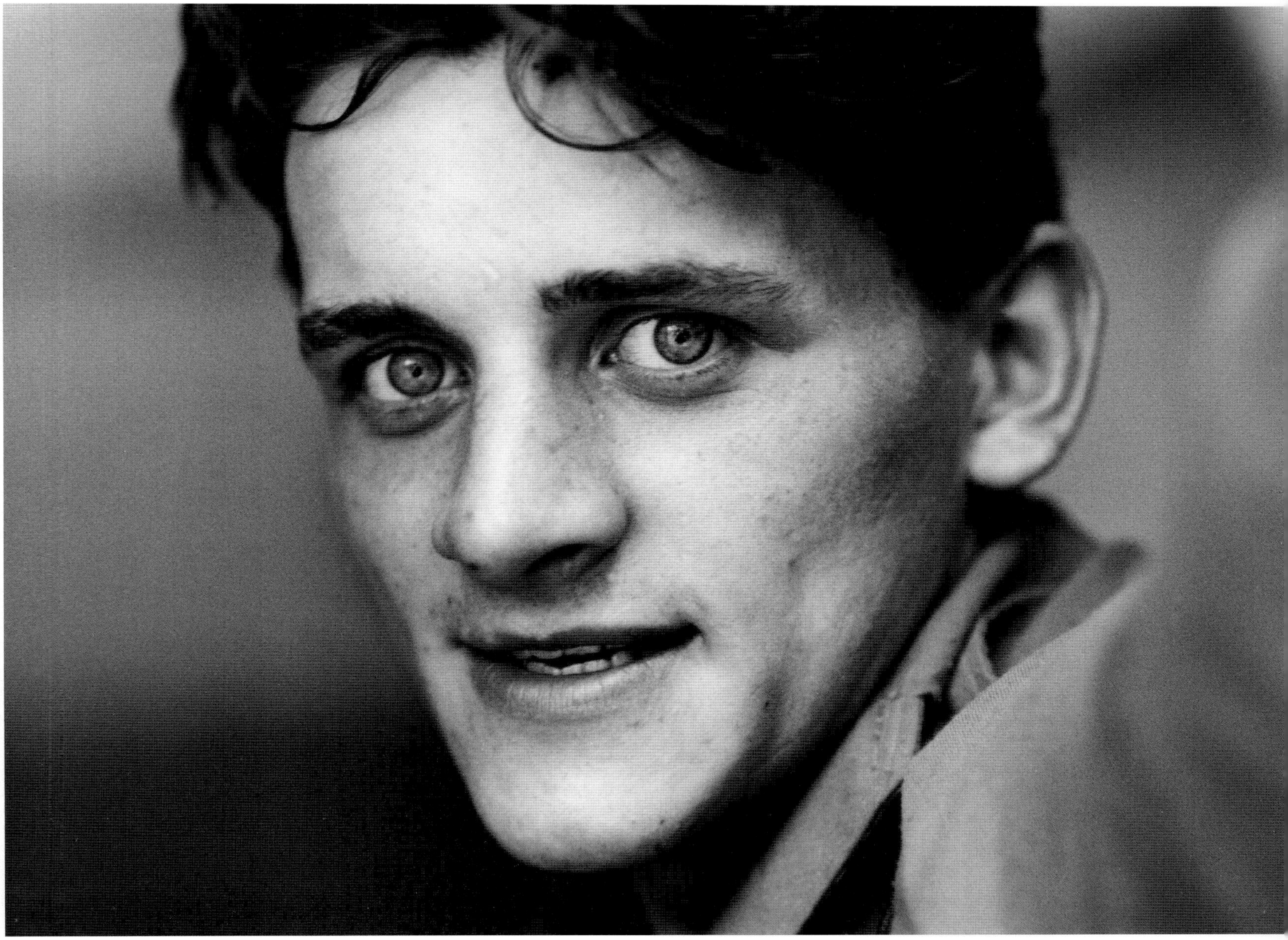

Prague 1992

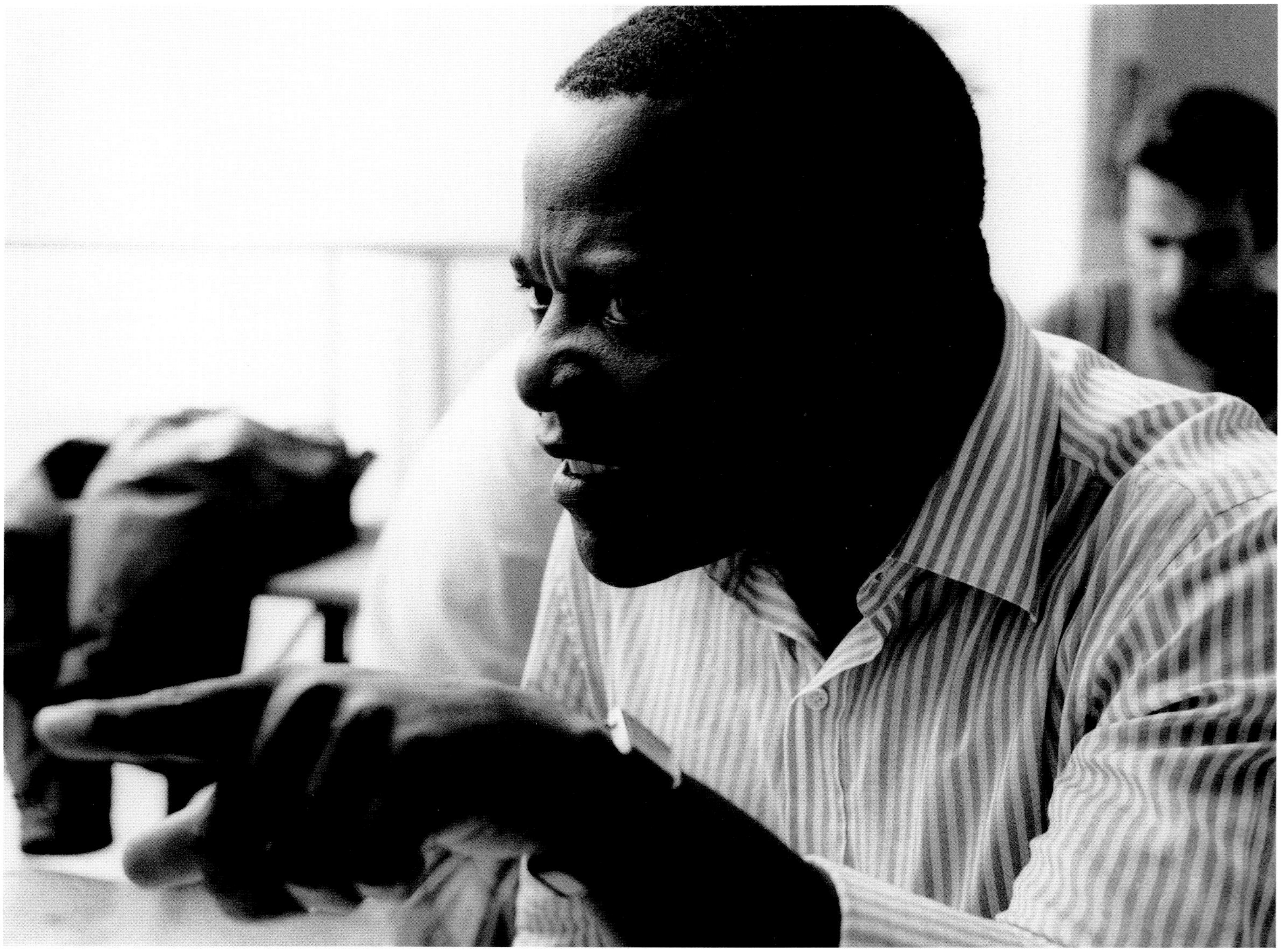

Munich 1991

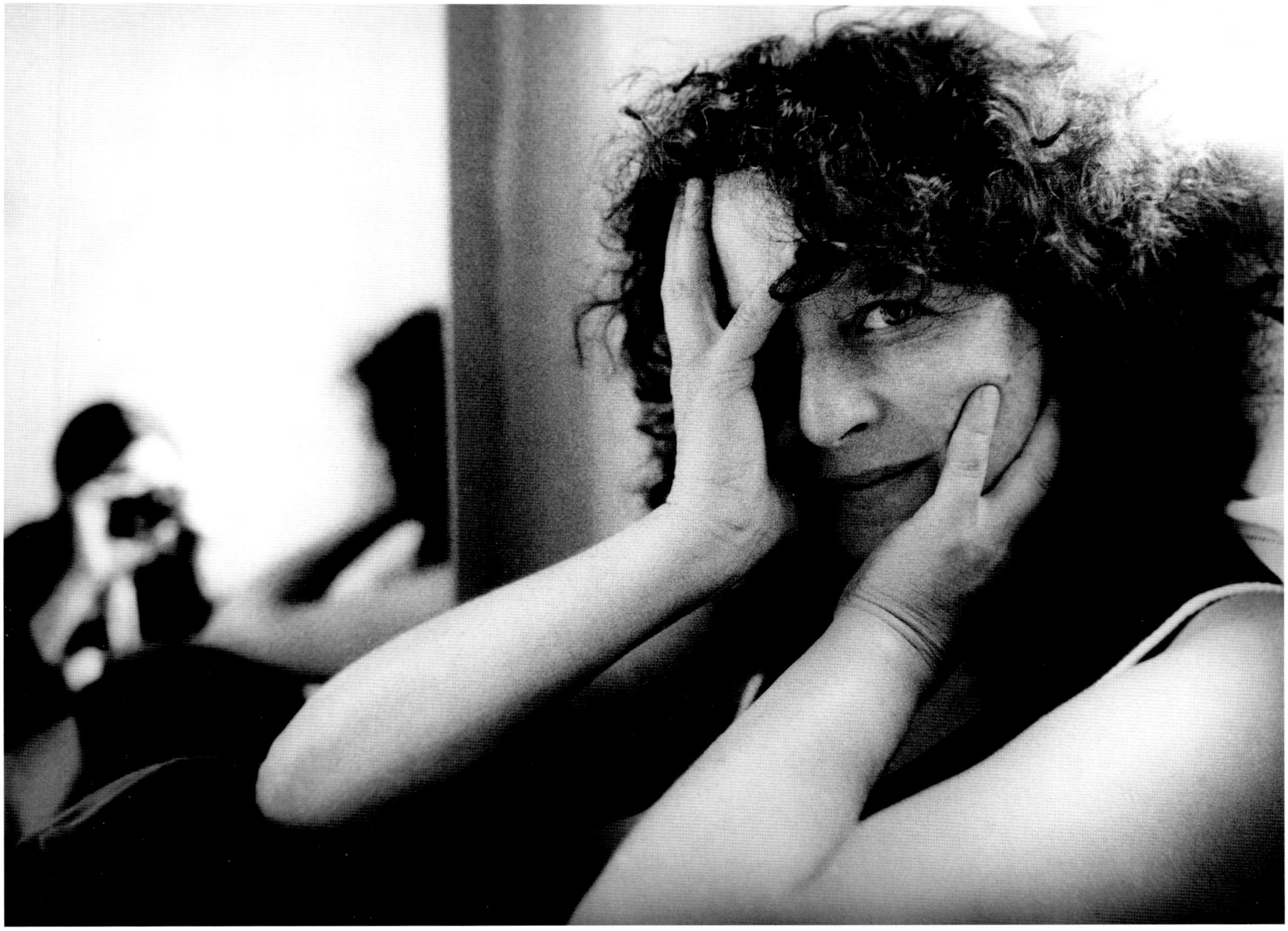

Schellerten 1999

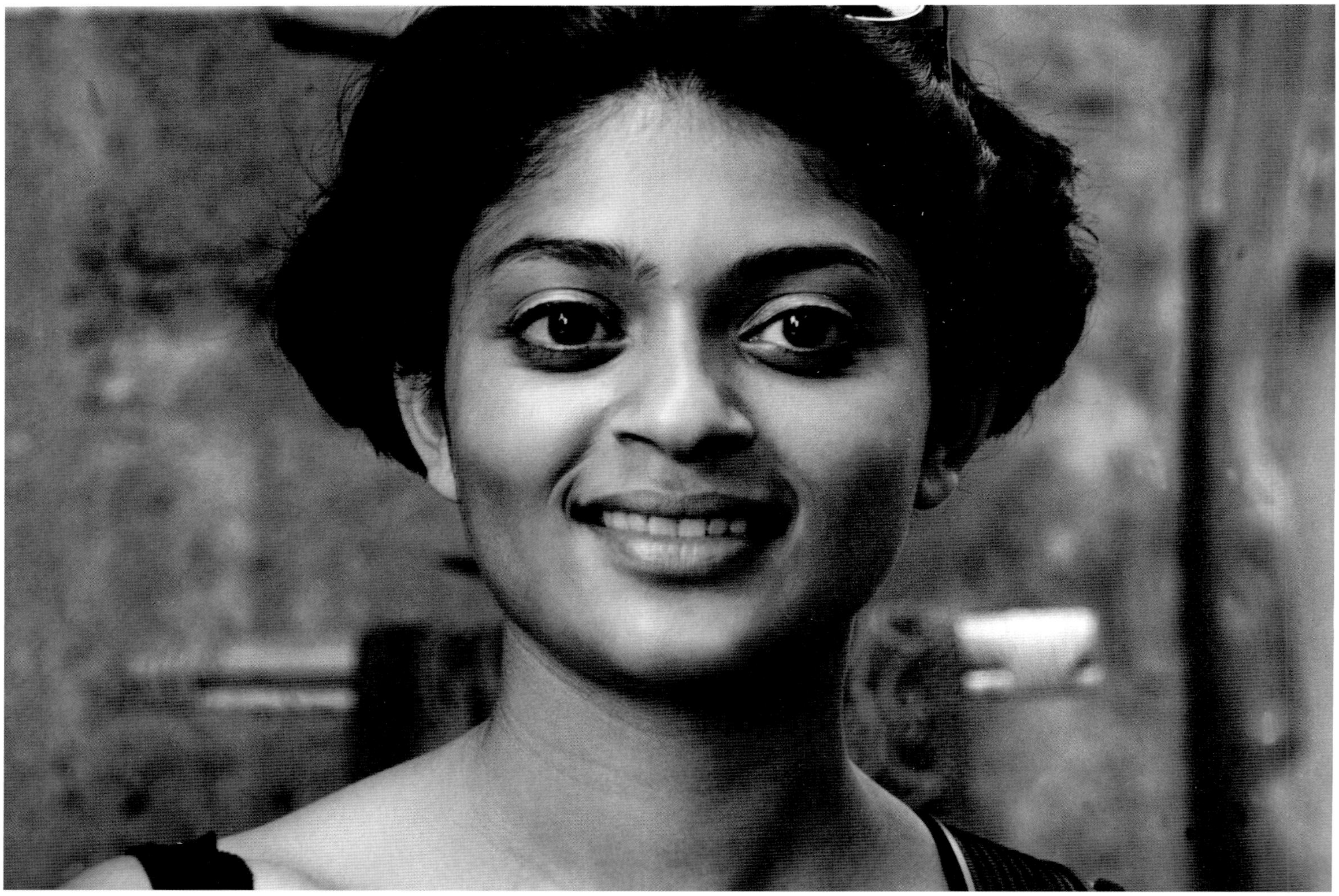

Los Angeles 1999

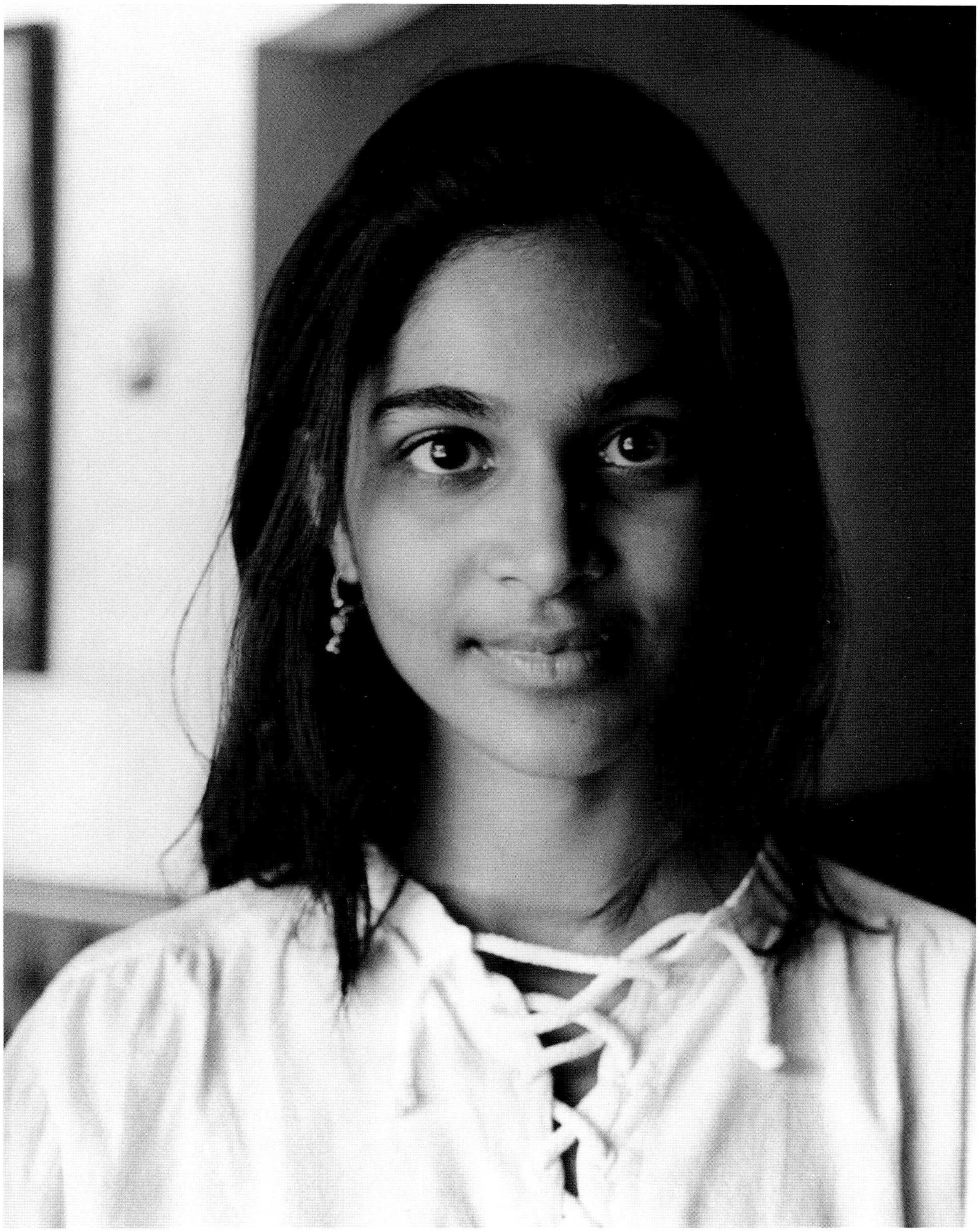

Hongkong 2000

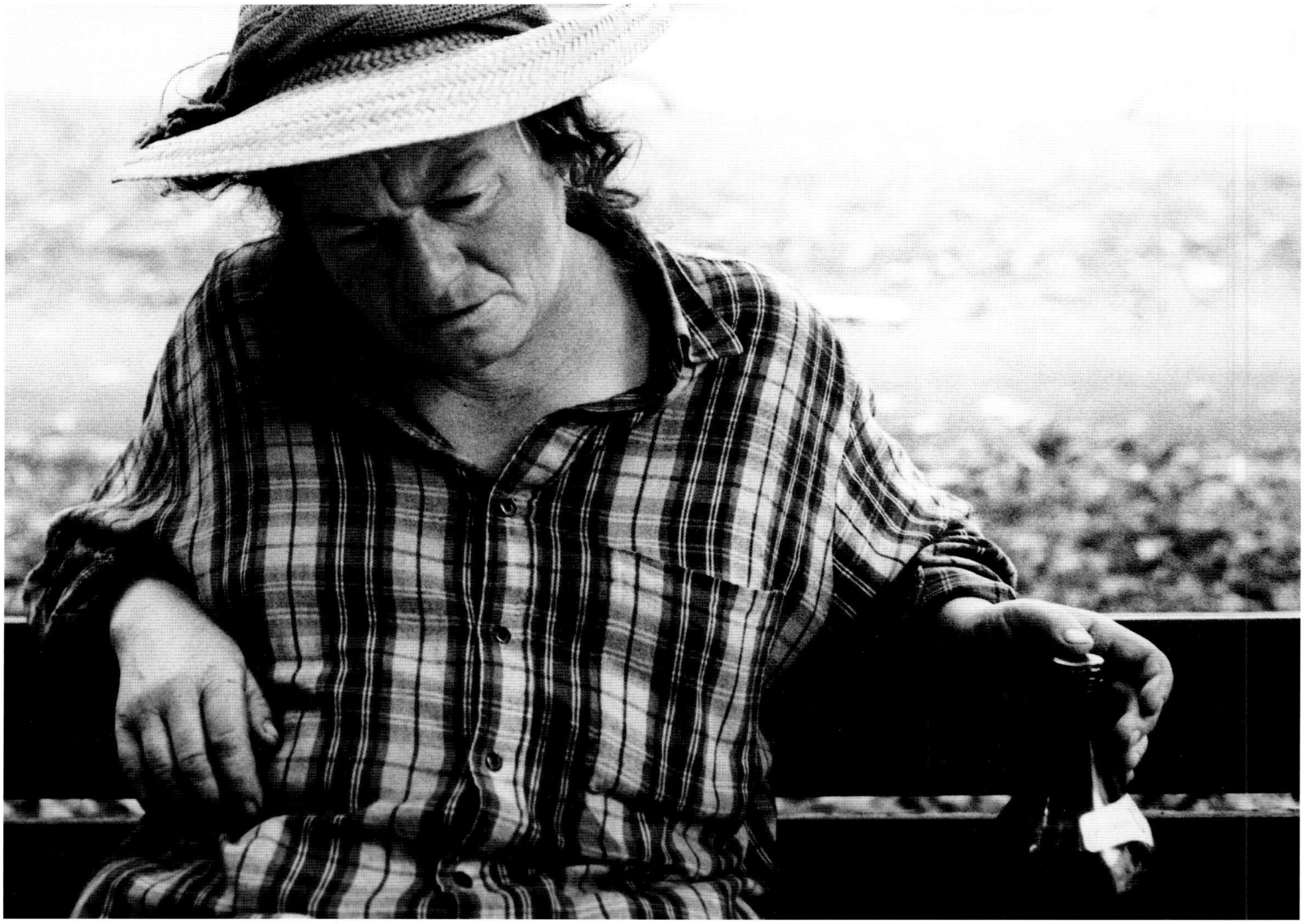

Munich 1999

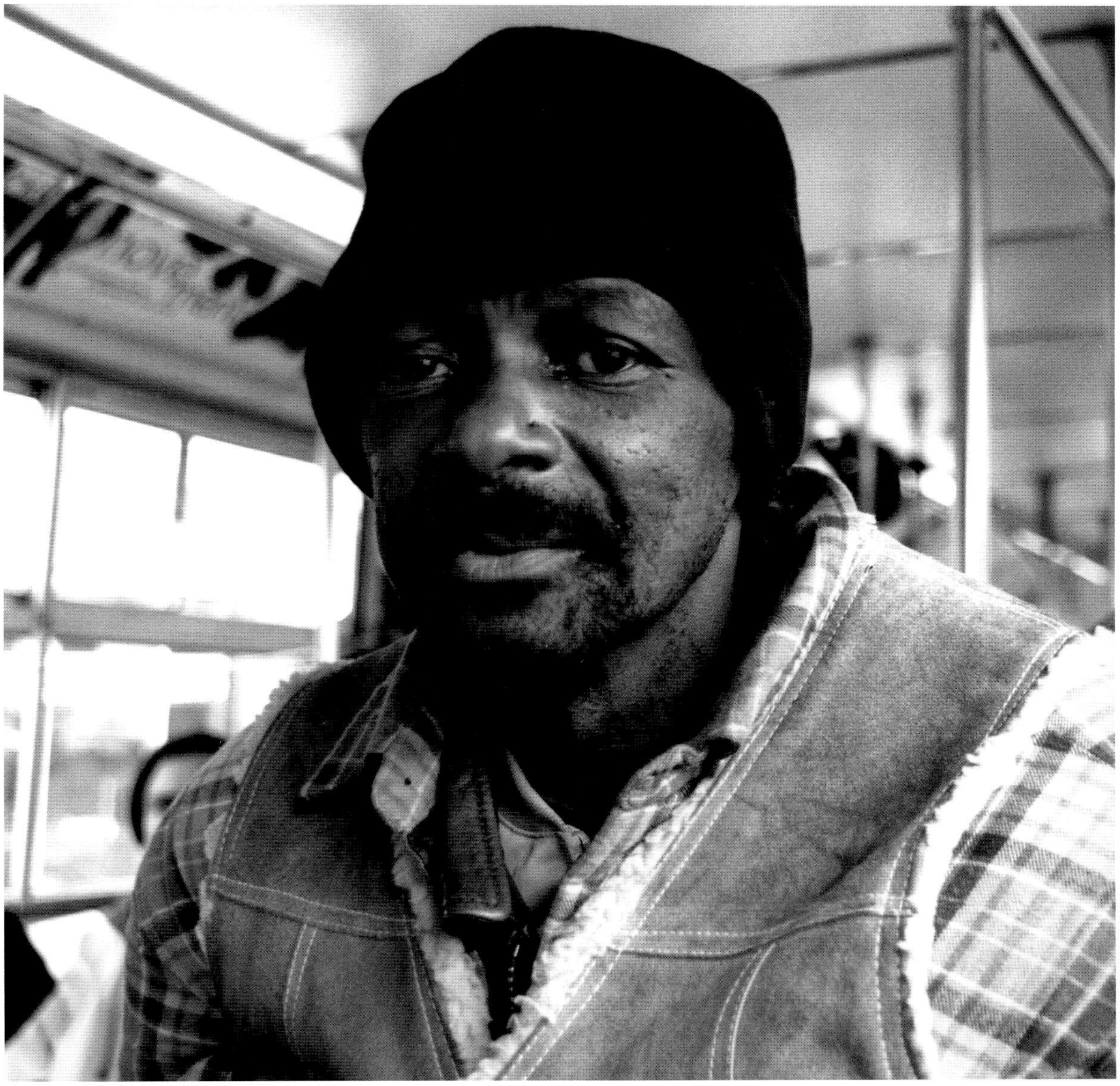

San Francisco 1999

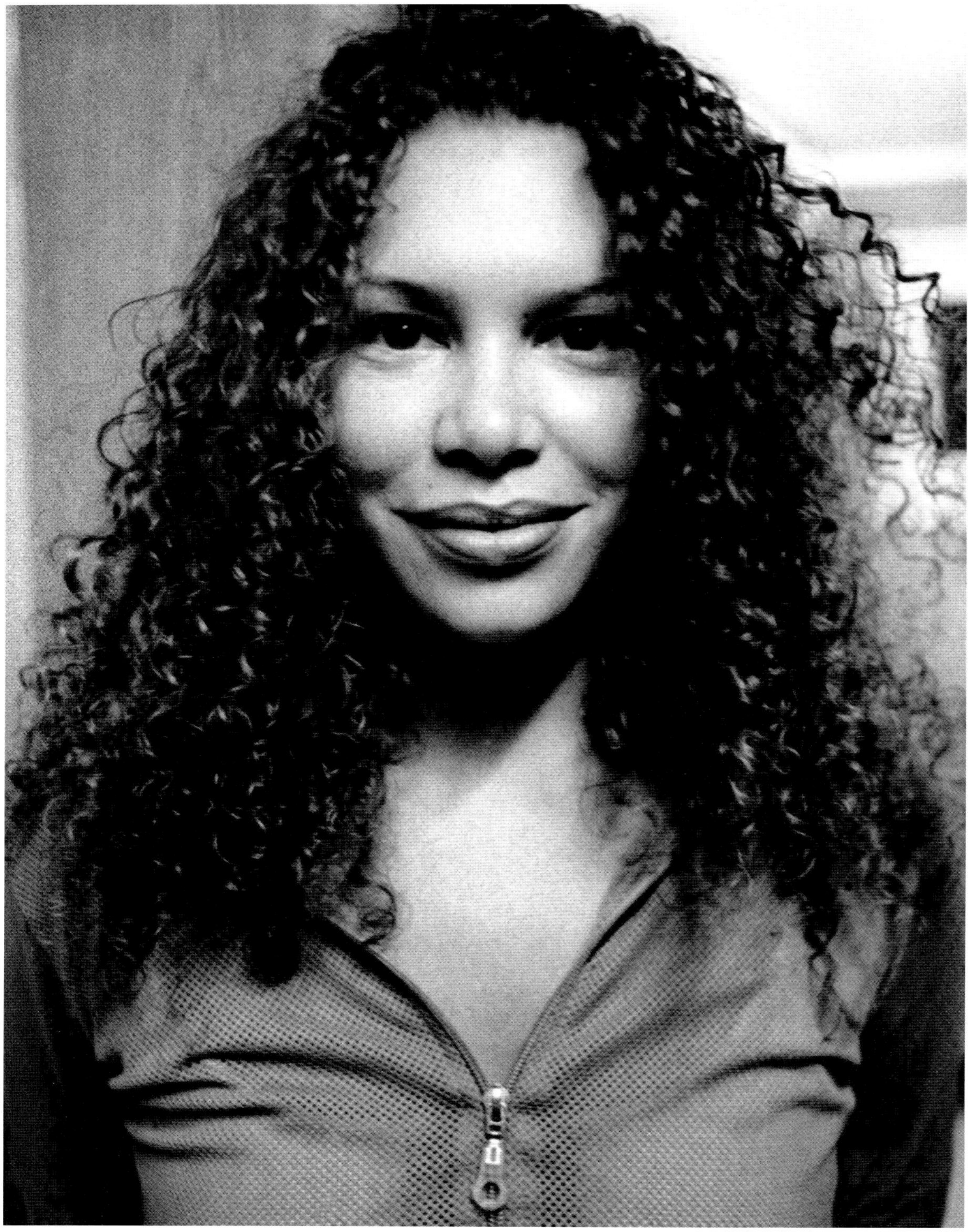

Sydney 1998

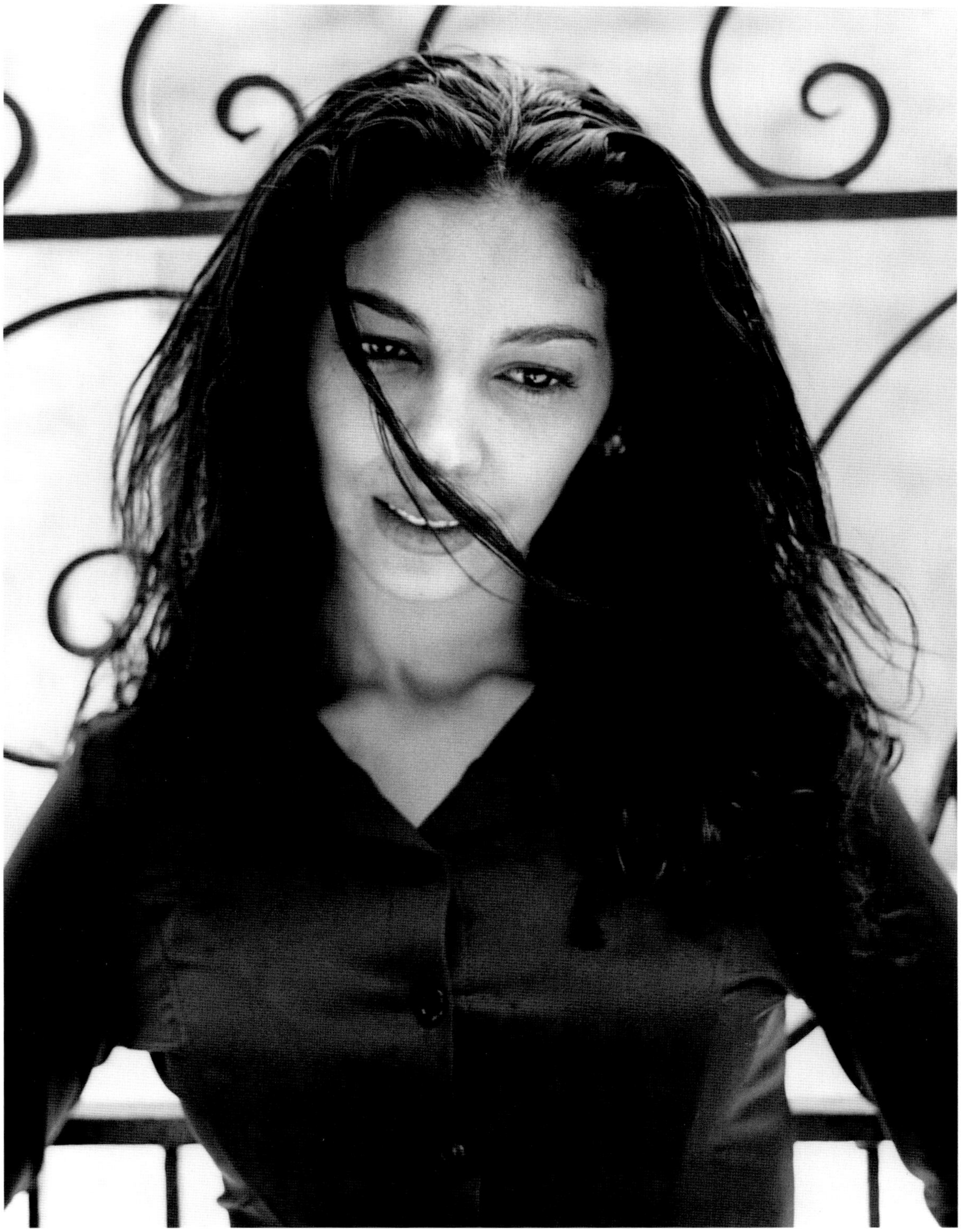

Arles 1999

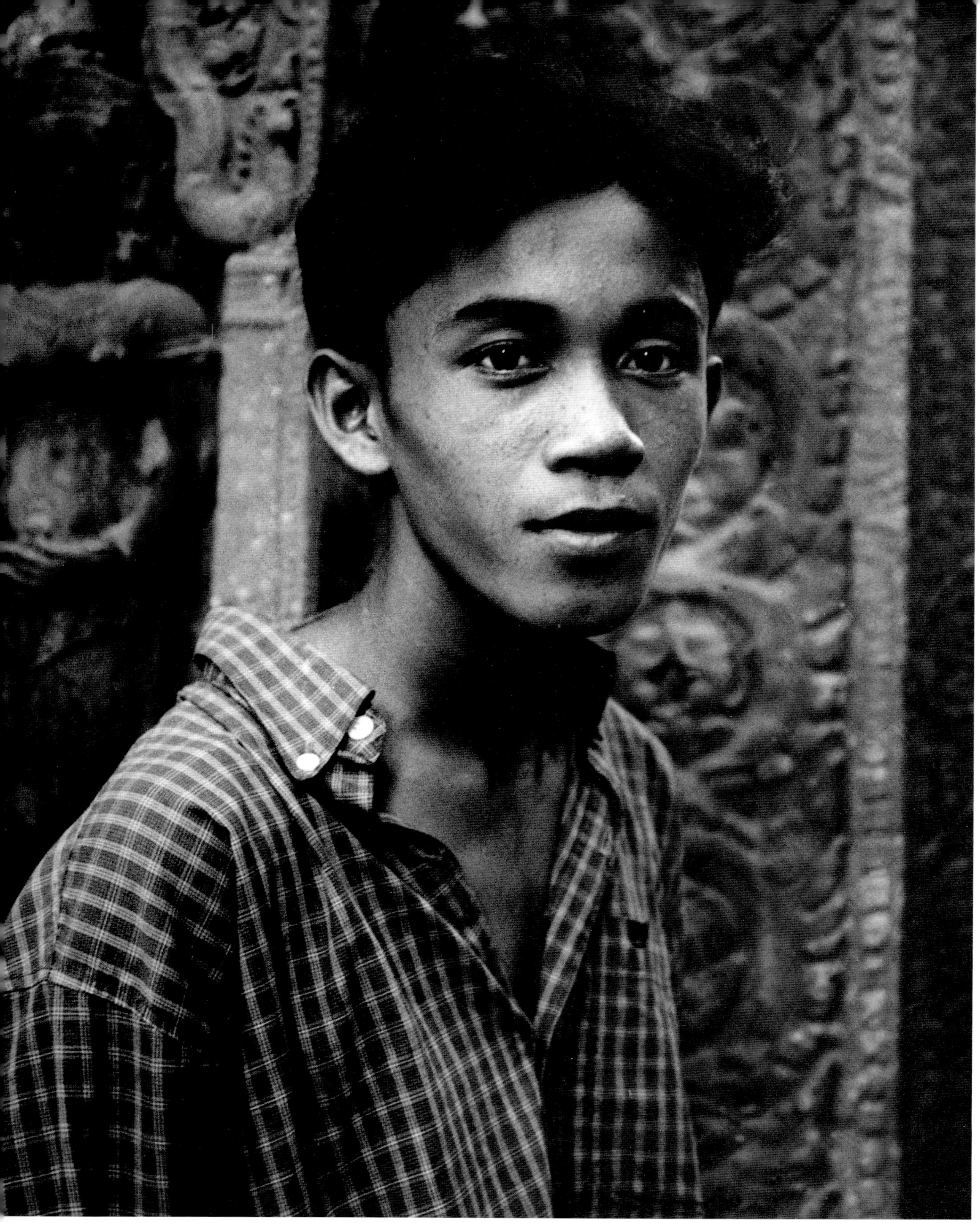

Angkor 2000

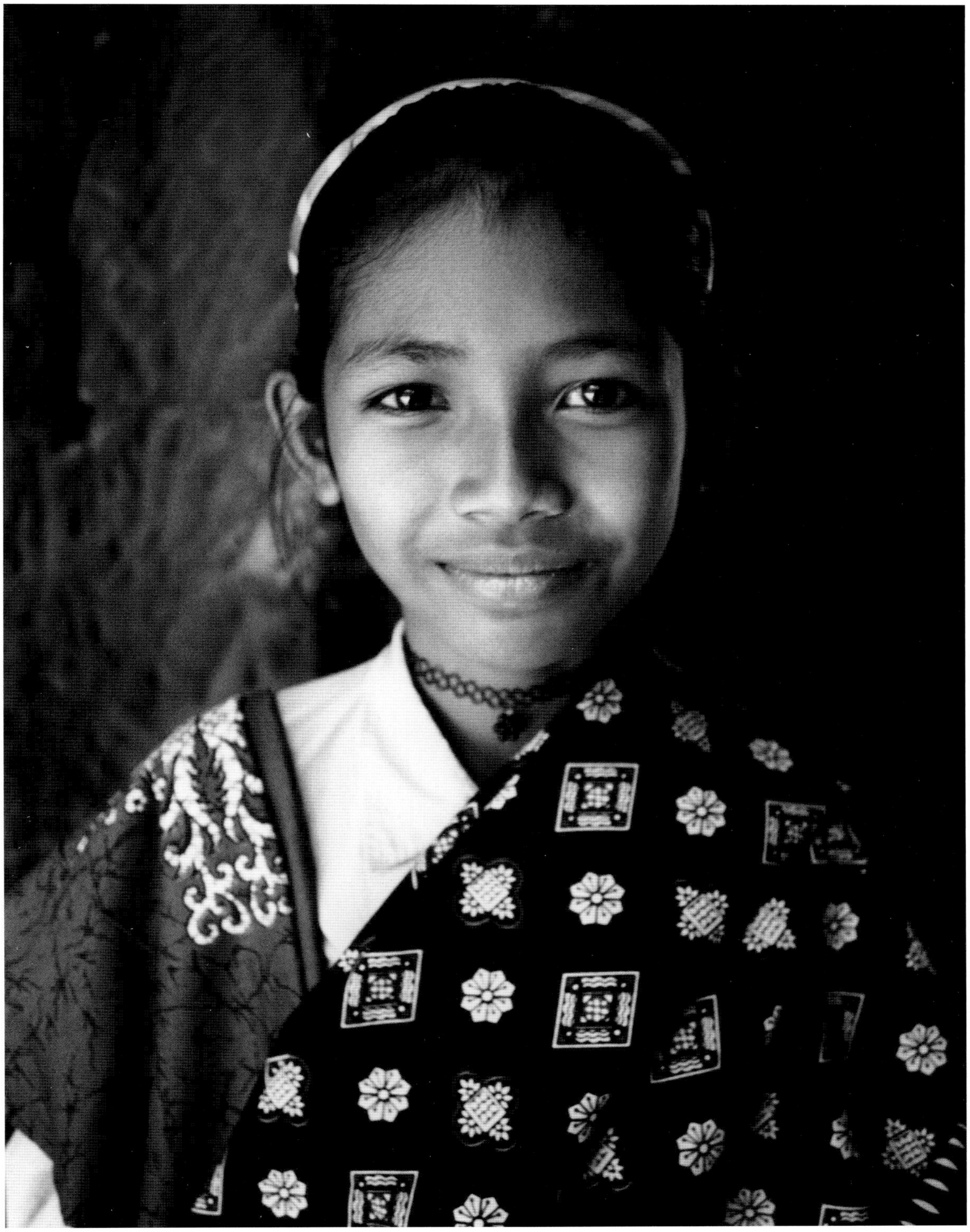

Angkor 2000

Xiao Hui Wang: A Biography

Projects · Exhibitions · Awards · Publications

Born in Tianjin, China, on 15 June, 1957.
Lives and works in Munich and Shanghai.

Educational Background

1978–86 Studied architecture at Tongji University, Shanghai, graduating in 1983; Master's degree thesis on 'Visual Information and its Communication'.

1986–87 Scholarship for advanced studies in Germany (Carl Duisberg Gesellschaft) and travel grant to study European architecture as a visiting scholar; continuation of architecture studies at the University of Technology, Munich.

1987–91 Work for doctoral thesis on 'The Conceptual Background of Classical Chinese Architecture'.

1990–92 Advanced studies in directing at the Academy for Film Studies, Munich.

Professional Experience

1986 Assistant lecturer at Tongji University, Shanghai.

1987–91 Assistant lecturer at the University of Technology, Munich.

1988–91 Lecturer at the Academy of Architecture in Munich for ancient Chinese architecture and garden architecture and history.

since 1991 Works as an artist-photographer and film-maker; regular member of the National Professional Artists' Association of Germany.

Architectural Projects

1985–86 Hotel project, Yangzhou (interior); planning and design of office buildings for the Jiuquan Steel Company; design and construction of restaurant in Shanghai in collaboration with the architect Yu Lin.

1987 Research programme on Shanghai buildings under Professor Baecher; exhibition at the international trade fair in Hanover.

Photography and Film Projects

1992 Script writer for Chinese sections ('Xian and Culture in Tang Dynasty', 'Emei Mountain and Buddhist Culture', 'Tai Mountain and Taoist Culture') in the television series *The Ancient Culture of the World*, produced by Bavaria Television.

1993 Consultant for the documentary film *Families in Beijing's Courtyard House*, a German and Chinese co-production.

1994 *The Broken Moon* (script, direction), a black-and-white 35 mm film; *The Chair*, a Chinese, Hong Kong and Japanese co-production (artistic supervisor, assistant director); directed and co-produced the documentary film *The Peking Opera Man at the End of the Century* (John Wate, co-director); participation at the International Photo Festival in Herten, Germany (lecture and exhibition).

1999 Photo workshop 'Capturing Feelings' at the International Photo Festival in Herten, Germany.

2001 Participation in the first 'Festival of Photography' in Asia, held in Dhaka, Bangladesh.

Exhibitions

One person shows (selection):

1990 'Licht und Widerschein', Werkbund Galerie, Berlin.

1992 'Xiao Hui Wang Photography', AGFA Center, Munich.

1993 'China Avant-garde', Haus der Kulturen der Welt, Berlin.

1997 Photographic Review, Art Museum Shanghai; 'Visual Diary and Associations with Death', International Photo Festival, Herten, Germany; 'Visual Diary etc.', Aktionsforum Praterinsel, Munich.

1998 'Contemporary Photo Art from China and Xiao Hui Wang', Kunsthalle Darmstadt; 'Frauenbilder', Photogalerie No Name, Basel.

1999 'Xiao Hui Wang Photography', Arts Center, Hong Kong; 'Frauenbilder und die neue Abstraktion', Haus der Fotografie, Hanover.

2001 'Close to the Eyes' – participant in the first festival of photography in Asia, Dhaka; 'Abstract Photography', Photogalerie in the Cultural Centre, Mannheim.

Group shows (selection):

1990 'Support Exhibition', Künstlerwerkstatt, Munich.

1998 'Century/Women', National Museum for Art, Beijing-'Gruber Exhibition', Photogalerie Lichtblick, Cologne.

1999 'Shanghai – In the Eyes of the World's Top Photographers', International Finance and Trade Center, Shanghai.

2001 'Die Schaukel', Das Gelbe Haus Museum, Flims, Switzerland.

Awards

1982–85 Received two national awards for architectural design competitions in China.

1986 University award for excellence in academic achievement.

1990 Nominated for Bavarian government grant.

1991 Nominated as 'Forum on Culture' artist by Munich Cultural Department.

1993 'Bayerische Filmförderung' award for the script *The Broken Moon*.

1994 Highest award ('Besonders Wertvoll') from Filmkuratorium Germany for *The Broken Moon*, Germany.

1995 Special award for *The Broken Moon*, at the International Film Festival in Bludenz, Austria.

1997 Received KODAK award: 'Works of Excellence' in China; nominated for the 'European Publishers Award for Photography '97'.

Publications (selection)

1991 *Sehen und Erleben*: München (photographs), Süddeutscher Verlag, Munich; *Heimat des Drachen* (text and photographs), Harenberg Edition, Dortmund; *Chinesische Klassische Architektur und Gartenbaukunst* (publication to accompany own series of seminars), Academy of Architecture, Munich.

1992 *Sehen und Erleben*: Sachsen (photographs), Süddeutscher Verlag, Munich; *Sehen und Erleben*: Prag (photographs), Süddeutscher Verlag, Munich.

1993 *Merian Live*: Bangkok (text and photographs), Gräfe und Unzer Verlag, Munich.

1995 *Blue Candle Burnt Out* (film script, published in Chinese), Shanghai; various film and television publications.

1997 *Frauenbilder* (photographs and text), Edition Braus, Heidelberg; *Wang Xiao Hui Photographic Review*, Earth Publishing and Printing Co., Hong Kong.

2000 *Architecture and its Communication* (in Chinese), Bai Hua Publishing, Tianjin; *Töchter des halben Himmels* (text with Monika Enders-Stamm and photographs), Fischer Verlag, Frankfurt; *Xiao Hui Wang: Abstract Photography*, Kehrer Verlag, Heidelberg.

2001 *My visual diary – 15 years in Germay* (in Chinese), Xuelin Publishing, Shanghai.

Contributions

1985 Feng Jicai: *100 People in 10 Years* (interviews about the Cultural Revolution), Literature and Art Publishing Jiansu, China.

1987 *How to live in Schanghai?* (publication accompanying research project under Prof. Baecher), Technical University, Darmstadt.

1990 *China der Frauen*, Frauenoffensive Verlag, Munich

1992 *Architecture and Literature* (text), China Architecture Publishing, Peking

1993 *China Avant-garde* (photographs), Cambridge University Press; *Keine Angst vor dünner Luft* (photographs, portraits of successful German women), Campus Press, Frankfurt/New York.

1997 'Internationale Fototage Herten', Edition Braus, Heidelberg.

1998 *Nude Photography: Masterpieces from the past 150 Years*, 60 selected photographs, Prestel Publishing, Munich, London, New York.

1999 *Shanghai: In the Eyes of the World's Top Photographers*, Shanghai Publishing.

2000 'World photographers focussing on Beijing', Beijing Foreign Cultural Exchange Service Center; 'First Festival of Photography in Asia', Dhaka; photographic work in Chinese Art Dictionary of the 20th Century, 70 selected photographers.

Work in progress

Children in Cambodia (photographs), proceeds from sales to be donated to Children's Aid in Cambodia; *Black Plants* (photographs), black-and-white photographs of plants and the human body; *Blumenseelen* (photographs), sensitive colour photographs of flowers.